FROM HILLSIDE TO
Farnborough Hill

FROM HILLSIDE TO
Farnborough Hill

125 YEARS OF THE
RCE IN FARNBOROUGH

Laura Craven and Laura Evans-Jones

THIRD MILLENNIUM
PUBLISHING, LONDON

From Hillside to Farnborough Hill:
125 years of the RCE in Farnborough
© Authors and Third Millennium Publishing Limited
First published in 2014 by
Third Millennium Publishing Limited, a subsidiary of
Third Millennium Information Limited

2–5 Benjamin Street
London
United Kingdom
EC1M 5QL
www.tmiltd.com

ISBN 978 1 908990 29 7

British Library Cataloguing in Publication Data
A CIP catalogue record for this book is available from the
British Library.

Editing: Val Horsler
Design: Helen Swansbourne
Production: Bonnie Murray and Debbie Wayment
Printed by: 1010 International Limited, China

PHOTOGRAPHIC CREDITS
Many of the photographs in the book come from the
school's archive, and have been much enhanced by
contributions from former pupils and staff. The school
and Third Millennium Publishing would also like to
thank Rolf Marriott, Martyn Poyner, Grant Pritchard and
Adam Catling for their modern photography.

Every effort has been made to contact copyright holders
and to obtain their permission for the use of material. In
the case of any inadvertent omission, please contact Third
Millennium Publishing; we will be pleased to correct any
errors in subsequent editions of this book.

Contents

Foreword

I t is my pleasure and privilege to write this Foreword as we celebrate the 125th anniversary of the education of girls (and for a few years, boys) by the Religious of Christian Education in Farnborough. The book is dedicated to all the Sisters (or Mothers, depending on your era at school) who devoted their lives to the care and education of young women so wholeheartedly and lovingly.

It is a tribute to the founding Sisters that the school is still thriving 125 years later; they were women of great vision and intellect as well as great faith. Much change has taken place under different headmistresses, but each has had to consider the circumstances in society at the time: the role of the Catholic church in people's lives, and the changing role of women. The curriculum on offer, and the nature of the pastoral care given to boarders and to day girls, have also varied, but at the school's heart has always been our mission of 'Educating the whole person in a caring Christian community'.

This book is not a history of the school although its chronology takes us through various episodes in history, most notably the two world wars. Rather, it is a collection of fascinating experiences, memories and anecdotes that celebrate the life of the school through the years. Its content owes a great deal to the school archives (kept meticulously by Sister Veronica Rennie) and the very informative school magazines. We are also grateful to the many 'old girls' and former members of staff who sent in various contributions for inclusion. Thanks must go to the authors, Laura Craven and Laura Evans-Jones (teachers in the English department), who have put their hearts into writing this book, and also to Clare Duffin who has spent many hours perusing photographs and other submissions to ensure that the very best have been included. What comes through in both the writing and the photographs is that while Farnborough Hill can be a 'quirky' place, it is also a very special place and those that have spent time here are all touched by it, and its Catholicity.

It is good to have a strong sense of the school's past but also essential that we have a clear vision for its future. When I have to make difficult decisions I often think to myself 'what would the Sisters have done?' It is, after all, their school and as we go forward we must retain all that is best from the past but also embrace all that is best for the future. I am confident that Farnborough Hill will continue, hopefully for another 125 years (at least), to prepare its students for whatever awaits them so that they can make a very positive mark on the world.

Sarah Buckle
Headmistress

1

The early years

The Longman house

In 1838 Thomas Longman, the publisher and owner of the London publishing houses 'The Ship' and 'The Black Swan', married Georgiana Bates. After having five daughters, they moved away from the city and in 1848 settled in Hampshire. In 1860, Thomas Longman demolished the old house on top of Windmill Hill and laid the foundation stone for his new house, which was completed in 1863. Unlike anything seen in Farnborough before, the Longman house was described both as 'that gabled monument of Victorian opulence' and 'a retreat as elegant as it is delightfully situated'. That original house remains at the core of the school today.

Empress Eugenie

Left: The original house in the Empress Eugenie's time

Above: Longman's publishing houses commemorated on the facade of the house

Doña María Eugenia Ignacia Augustina de Palafox-Portocarrero de Guzmán y Kirkpatrick, 16th Countess of Teba and 15th Marquise of Ardales, is better known to us at Farnborough Hill simply as Empress Eugenie. Born on 5 May 1826 in Granada, Spain, she was brought up and educated mostly in France where, in 1849, at a reception at the Elysée Palace, she met Prince Louis Napoleon. Their engagement was formally announced by Louis himself on

Left: Empress Eugenie in a portrait of 1853

Far left: The Empress with her husband, Napoleon III, and their only son, 1860s

22 January 1853 after he had become Emperor Napoleon III, and they were married in a civil ceremony at the Tuileries on 29 January 1853 with a much larger nuptial mass at Notre Dame the following day. They had one son, Napoleon Eugene Louis Jean Joseph Bonaparte, who became known as the Prince Imperial.

After France's defeat in the Franco-Prussian war, Louis and Eugenie were exiled to Camden Place in Chislehurst, Kent, where Louis died on 9 January 1873 during surgery to remove a bladder stone, leaving Eugenie bereft. When this tragedy was further compounded in 1879 by the death of the Prince Imperial during the Anglo-Zulu War, Eugenie was devastated. Her desire to build a memorial chapel at Chislehurst for their tombs was met with refusal by the landowner, prompting a search for a new home with a suitable resting place for her husband and son. In 1880, she bought Farnborough Hill and, after extensive renovation and development, moved there in 1882. She divided her time between Hampshire and the Villa Cyrnos which she had built on the Cote d'Azur as a retirement home untarnished by familial memories. The Winter Garden (which still exists today as home to the junior fiction section of the library) was built onto the original Longman house to allow space for Eugenie to grieve for her beloved husband and son. From her favourite seat in the window, she could see across the grounds to the mausoleum at Farnborough Abbey where they were finally laid to rest.

The Empress maintained a close friendship with Queen Victoria through their marriages and subsequent widowhoods, and Victoria visited Eugenie at Farnborough Hill several times (see box). The Empress also had a long association with the nuns and the school, then at Hillside, often having groups of girls for afternoon tea with her own family and frequently presiding at the annual prize giving, held in French in her honour. According to Carla Davis (Roantree), Mother Roantree spoke 'excellent French which she used to great effect when she met the Empress Eugenie at Farnborough and they became friends. Some of the girls from the school in the town were invited to tea with the Empress on Sundays at her grand house on the hill.'

With her health declining, Eugenie took what was to be her final trip to her native Spain in July 1920 where she died, surrounded by her family and at peace with her faith. Her body travelled through Spain and France in full royal state, and was taken to Farnborough Abbey where she was finally laid to rest alongside her beloved husband and son.

Abbé Lafosse

Louis Francois Marin Lafosse was born in 1772, the sixth of seven children of a Catholic farming family in Montreuil-au-Houlme. The religious turbulence of the Revolution bedevilled his vocation as a priest – he even spent some time in prison – but he was eventually able to resume a full

The bust of Abbé Lafosse in the lower refectory

From Queen Victoria's diaries

28 SEPTEMBER 1880: [The Empress is] buying for £50,000 the property of Farnborough Hill, quite close to the Farnborough station and Aldershot, with a good new house, hot houses, stables etc – fine grounds 257 acres and a fine position, on high ground. I am so glad of this.

30 JUNE 1882: The dear Empress Eugenie arrived from Farnborough Hill, where she has been staying, since the end of May, in a great state of discomfort, but was determined to expedite the works, which she has succeeded in doing.

7 MARCH 1884: Reached Farnborough Hill at quarter to two. One drives in at a lodge... through pretty ground, up to the house, which looks imposing, with a tower. It is an irregular building of white brick, with wooden beams and gabled roofs, in the old English style. The Empress took us through the hall, in which hangs the celebrated picture of her and her ladies by Winterhalter, into a small room, arranged as a dressing room, but which is her boudoir... We lunched in a beautiful dining room at the end of a fine corridor, also entirely built by her and added on.

[Queen Victoria visited the Empress at Farnborough several more times, always accompanied by her daughter Princess Beatrice and

An engraving of the house from the sale catalogue of 1880

sometimes also by Beatrice's husband, Prince Henry of Battenberg, known as Liko, as well as by other members of the family and household.]

1 DECEMBER 1892: Left at quarter to one for Farnborough Hill... The Empress was all kindness and wonderfully well. The cure at Bath has made her quite active again. If I only could become so too. But unfortunately I cannot stand baths. [After lunch] I sat with her whilst the others went to see the chapel.

ministry in the Catholic church. He always believed in the value of schooling for both boys and girls, focusing on the use of up-to-date books and methods and on giving his pupils a solid foundation for their Christian lives. This led to the starting of an ecclesiastical school where he prepared some boys for training for the priesthood. But he always felt that the education of girls was being overlooked, and so began to look for female volunteers to become teachers. Four young women – Marie-Anne Dutertre, Victoirie Buisson, Rose Gibory and Marie-Louise Mahloire – agreed to train under his guidance and instruction and, responding to God's call to a religious vocation, sought permission to fulfil their teaching mission as religious. On 21 November 1817, in a small church in Echauffour, north-west France, those first four pioneering women took vows of poverty, chastity and obedience and made their profession to become the first Sisters of the Religious of

Christian Education. Abbé Lafosse had had no intention of founding a religious congregation, but when he died at Echauffour on 21 December 1839 he left a rich legacy, not only to the parish he had served so faithfully and courageously but also to generations of girls throughout the world who have attended an RCE school.

Despite these small and humble beginnings – the Sisters lived in poverty out of necessity in post-revolutionary France, using the presbytery as their convent and the village church as their chapel – the Order grew swiftly, and by the time of their founder's death, fifty-three girls had taken their vows. Moreover, his wish that they should become teachers bore fruit very early in their history. In 1819, only two years after the first profession ceremony, the parish priest in Argentan asked the Sisters to set up a school in his parish, and this was followed by similar requests from other towns. In 1838 the Sisters were given funds to found a teacher

The first three pupils at Hillside, Susanna Murray, Marie Majorie and Josephine Murray, together with Mother Caroline Murray, her sister, Mme de Villalonga and Sister Secords. Mother Murray was one of the trio of nuns who founded the school in Farnborough, and this is the first photograph of the school

training college for women in Argentan, the first of its kind in France, an implicit approval of the RCE as a teaching Order. There, as in all the houses, the atmosphere was homely with a strong focus on relaxed, friendly relationships between Sisters and students, both past and present.

But there were difficulties, rooted in the anti-clericalism of the French Revolution and finding expression in the rapid movement in France, throughout the nineteenth century, towards the permanent separation of church and state. The teaching communities were left with two choices – find a legal way to get around the anti-clerical laws, or migrate somewhere safer and more secure.

1880 saw the election as Superior-General of Euphanie Duval, 'a woman of vision and strength, who viewed difficulties as problems to be overcome and persecution as a challenge to expand the Congregation apostolically and geographically'. This determination and strength of spirit were exactly what was needed to guide the RCE through this difficult time. As the anti-clerical laws took hold, an increasing number of RCE schools were being closed down, which left many Sisters in need of redeployment. It was decided that emigration was the best option for the safe continuance of the Order.

Mother Duval started investigating the possibility of moving at least some of the Order to England in the autumn of 1886, when Mother Murray's brother, Lieutenant-Colonel Robert Murray, who had been stationed at Aldershot Barracks, suggested that somewhere around the Aldershot area would be a safe, peaceful and appropriate place for the nuns to settle. In 1889 Mother Duval and Mother Murray received approval from the Bishop of Portsmouth to search for a property within his diocese in which they would begin an English branch of the RCE. When she visited Farnborough, Mother Duval's heart became set on one particular house, 'small but sufficient for the new foundation, with an attractive garden and pine woods adjoining it'. Hillside was part of the estate of General Gordon, who had been killed in Khartoum in 1885, and at that time was not for sale. Before returning to France, the two nuns extracted a promise from their land agent that he would inform them as soon as anything else suitable became available. Within a week they received a telegram: 'Hillside for sale'. Mother Duval replied with an apparently highly characteristically short message: 'Buy property at once, arriving...'.

The Murray family

On 5 January 1958 Josephine Murray died at Rainham, Essex, in her eighty-first year. Not only was she the very first pupil of the school but her family was closely bound up with the history of the foundation in Farnborough.

The Earl of Tullibardin, Lord James Murray, and his family were forced into exile after the Jacobite rebellion of 1745 and settled in France. He had several children, one of whom, Anthony, married Mary Orr and produced another large family, including Robert and Caroline. Caroline became a nun in the Order at Argentan and was instrumental in persuading her brother Robert to facilitate the move from France to Farnborough. Robert was a high-ranking officer in the British army stationed at Farnborough and agreed with his sister about the need for a school which would cater for the children of serving officers; he was himself the father of nine children.

His daughter, Josephine, was already a student with the Sisters at Argentan and subsequently became the first student at Hillside when it opened in May 1889. Her sister Justina also subsequently joined the new school in Farnborough. As her godson, Tony Murray, recalled: 'Josephine was the eldest daughter and a very bright student – she won an award from the Empress Eugenie. She never married, but did travel in Spain for several years as her aunt was married to the Marquis de Villalonga. She was, at the time, what might be called a bit of a firebrand and while in Spain ran off with a matador. In complete

Members of the Murray family pictured in 1939 with Mother Fehrenbach. Josephine Murray, the first pupil, is second from the left

contrast, her younger sister Justina entered the congregation and joined the community at Farnborough. By all accounts, Justina's fate was sealed by my great-grandfather as a result of Josephine's exploits! I think it should be noted that life for women back then was very different – in my family it was marriage or the nunnery for girls. As is now known, Justina went on to become a doyenne of the community. She is remembered hugely fondly by our family, but I do sometimes think that my dearest godmother would have loved to have lived in the world your girls live in today with all of its opportunities for women. We are so proud of Justina and her passion about empowering women through education through her work at Hillside and Farnborough Hill.'

Girls demonstrating hockey and tennis skills at Hillside, c 1900

Hillside

On 30 April 1889, a cold and miserable day, Mothers Murray, Roantree and Desroullers came to Farnborough. After spending the night as guests of the monks at St Michael's Priory (now Farnborough Abbey), they went to Hillside. They were met at the foot of the steps by Old Cook, the gardener, with his hat in one hand and the keys in the other.

The diary of the foundation describes how the nuns slept that night under curtains and old rugs which they had collected to take the place of the blankets that had not arrived; how excited they were on that first day of May to receive letters from the Mother House and the Reverend Mother General, who seemed so far away; how, when the nuns had gone to Mass at the Priory the next morning, Colonel Murray had lit the fire for them and was found sweeping the kitchen when they came back, while 'Little Joe' opened the door to them, beaming with delight at their surprise; how they breakfasted then, drinking out of broken cups and a pudding basin, having as yet no supply of furniture or crockery.

First Impressions

A poem from a new boarder at Hillside

I wandered lonely as a cloud
Through corridors and classrooms neat
When all at once I saw a crowd
A host of girls upon a seat
Beside a lawn, beneath the trees
Sewing industriously in the breeze.
Continuous as the stars that shine
And twinkle in the Milky Way
The minutes stretched as I did pine
For home upon that dreary day
I wept and wept but little thought
What sense that day to me had brought.
For oft as in my bed I lie
In vacant or in pensive mood
I think of what a fool am I
And wonder how I ever could
Have been so wretched on that day
For now I am as gay as gay.

A gas lamp at Hillside, 1920s

Farnborough. Hillside Co

Two more Sisters arrived on 3 May, one of whom was Mother Duplanck who was to become the first Superior of the new foundation. They brought with them a young French girl, Marie Majorie, sent by her family to learn English. On 15 May, Hillside opened. The first pupil was Josephine Murray, who had been there with the Sisters since they arrived at Hillside, and the first 'day boarder' was May Wallis who, even in her nineties, was one of Farnborough Hill's most regular visitors.

Day boarders were at school from 9am until 7pm which helped create the 'esprit de famille' that the Sisters spoke of so fondly. Mother Roantree described how they were soon joined by two other boarders, 'a happy trio', as well as eight further day pupils, all of whom soon 'seemed to find themselves part of the family'.

Numbers grew steadily, and in 1892 the Sisters began to build a new chapel at Hillside in order to accommodate their pupils. The foundation stone was laid by the Bishop of Portsmouth, Dr Vertue, on 17 July 1893 and the chapel opened and was dedicated in the spring of 1895. By 1899 there were so many boarders that land was bought across the road to become St Mary's Day School for the ever-increasing number of day pupils. By 1907 there were over eighty boarders, necessitating the building of another wing which contained the refectory (later to

Above: Hillside, 1909. The original house on the left belonged to General Gordon of Khartoum. The middle block with tower was designed by Mr Hansom of cab fame

Below: A page from Eileen O'Dowd Egan's autograph book, 1908

Ode on a Motor Car
Stinkle, stinkle, little car.
How I wonder if you are
always going to smell so high.
As you stinkle, stinkle by.

Hillside. April 14th 1908.

I remember going to Hillside for the summer term 1903 when I was just six years old. There were only six of us in the class and one of them was the Honourable Constance Knot who was always getting into trouble. The Empress Eugenie patronised our school and gave a silver reward for the best girl in the seniors, junior and prelim classes. My eldest sister, Molly O'Dowd Egan, won all three. Being the youngest in the school I had the honour of presenting the Empress with a bouquet for which I was given a kiss, so I feel I have a bit of history attached to me, as I must be the only person alive who was kissed by her. In the middle of the summer terms we had our yearly picnic and I remember the big horse-drawn brake that took us to where we were going. One year we went on the Thames to Windsor Castle. The nuns were called Madame in my time at school. There were three families with four sisters in my second last year: the McAuliffes, the Barretts and the O'Dowd Egans.
Eileen O'Gorman Quin (O'Dowd Egan), letter 20 April 1989

Empress Eugenie and prize giving

Thursday last was the annual prize giving at the Convent of Our Lady of the Sacred Heart, Hillside, Farnborough, when the Empress Eugenie kindly consented to present the prizes. Her Majesty, who was accompanied by Prince Victor Napoleon, the young Marquis de Castillon and his mother, Madame le Breton, and other ladies, was received by the Reverend Mother at the gate, the pupils lining each side of the drive, all dressed in cream frocks, and several wearing the blue ribbons and medals obtained by good conduct. After a close inspection of the various articles of plain and fancy needlework, painting, drawing, embroidery and ornamental writing, which did great credit both to mistresses and pupils, the visitors entered the drawing room and, after an address of welcome to Her Majesty had been read by the eldest French girl, a pretty charade called 'Birds and Fairies' was acted. Then, when each girl's name was called, the Empress, with a kiss, gave her a handsomely bound book; some winning three or four. Besides these, Her Majesty gave a special prize of honour, chosen by herself, to the best girl in each of the three divisions of the school as elected by her companions. These consisted of a writing case, a lady's companion (both in Russia leather) and a travelling clock; the lucky recipients of which were also crowned by the Empress with white roses. Their names are Miss Teresa Dowling, Miss May Wallis and Miss Cissie McCaffrie. It is rather curious that they are natives of the three sister countries: England, Ireland and Scotland. After listening with evident pleasure to the well-rendered songs, duets and recitations by the pupils, the Empress and suite drove back to Farnborough Hill, leaving a happy party of girls preparing to enjoy their well-earned holiday.

Prize giving programme, 1904

Above: From Anna Lefebvre's prayer book, 1896. She was born in Lille and educated at Hillside 1890–8

become a gymnasium), a concert hall, music rooms, art and craft rooms and a large dormitory which would later become a needlework room alongside a geography room. After Reverend Mother Duplanck's move to America in 1907, Mother Roantree, who had been Mother Duplanck's assistant and directress of studies ever since the foundation,

became Superior with Mother Duchemin as her assistant. As Mother Roantree wrote in 1909: 'In the old days the girls worked hard, God bless them! And the seed they sowed of honest, earnest work has borne fruit in each succeeding generation. To this day it would be difficult to find a more thorough set of girls. Whether it be study or games, they put

The 1917 school fete. Mother Roantree with Princess Clementine, Madame D'Atanville (niece of the Empress) and Judge Law-Smythe. The fete was opened by the Lord Mayor and Lady Mayoress of London

The First World War

The outbreak of war in 1914 did not unduly affect the community at Hillside until their buildings were commandeered by the military in 1915. Both the boarding and day schools were temporarily closed and Mother Ward with her community and day pupils migrated to Chudleigh in Victoria Road, Farnborough, while the older boarders went with Mother Agnes Murray, Mother Tombret and a number of other nuns to Leehurst, near Salisbury, a recently opened RCE foundation. The majority of the Hillside community, including twenty junior and middle school boarders, moved to The Sycamores in Farnborough Park in November 1915. Having been a family house, Sycamores was not entirely suited to school life and 'for a year or more, the builders were constantly in the house, adding to it, roofing in courtyards and building on waste spaces and adapting it to its new dignity as a convent school'. However, they 'made do', turning the drawing room into their chapel and installing the treasured statue of Our Lady of the Sacred Heart. It was at this point that the tradition began for the daily recitation of the prayer 'Souvenez-vous O Notre Dame du Sacre Coeur' which continued to be said regularly

their hearts into what they do. The studies and the games have both advanced, and each succeeding year has brought some improvements such as we of twenty years ago never dreamed of. However, we made the best of what we had, and our advice to the present generations is to do likewise and to learn as we did the truth of our motto: "In Domino labor vester non est inanis".'

It requires a certain amount of imagination, even on my part (who has had the privilege of watching our alma mater grow from its small beginning), to visualise the first Hillside as it was in 1891 when it opened its doors to me, its first day boarder. There were then about thirteen boarders and a handful of nuns occupying merely one side of the present three-square building, the house that is now called St Joseph's. I wonder how many of our readers can remember the first, and at the time the only, visiting professor, Mr Thomas of music fame, and how we never went to singing class without gloves. What a happy lot of girls we were! So friendly to each other and so devoted to our dear nuns. There was the delightful mixture of nationalities, Irish,

English and French – so good for our characters, as well as for the opportunities it afforded of learning two languages in a colloquial way without any sense of drudgery.

Certain feasts and holidays were looked forward to with great eagerness, and each term brought us its different celebration. To begin with, St Patrick very often gave us a beautiful spring day for his feast, which meant we could have a long walk, the destination of which was our choosing, and then a grand play or concert in the evening. The summer term brought us the feast of Corpus Christi with the Altar of Repose in our dear old wood, where, too, we always spent our recreation in fine weather. In the Christmas term there was the feast of the Immaculate Conception, on

which there was a reception of Children of Mary, generally followed by a jolly evening. Sandwiched between these feasts were the shorter holidays such as half-day for Shrove Tuesday. This will recall to some of my contemporaries the enormous bottles of sweets we could buy at Hitchcock's in those days (fetched by the ever faithful Joli) and yet demolish them before Ash Wednesday dawned. Oh yes! And what about the pancakes which flowed on and on from kitchen to refectory like the proverbial brook until Madame Delrue's arms being in danger of falling off after so much tossing, she called for volunteers, and the first class girls were allowed to help, to the envy of all the others.
May Wallis

The Sycamores. *Above*, an engraving of the west front 1925; *far left and below*, the entrance hall and a reception room in the early 1920s; and *left*, the tennis courts, 1933

by nuns and girls alike for many years as the school celebrated the feast day of the Sacred Heart.

September 1916 saw the return of the senior boarders from Salisbury. Despite the war, numbers were still growing; so, with over 200 day pupils needing teaching as well as the boarders, Wymering Lodge was purchased. Along with a number of army huts on the lawn between the lodge and Sycamores, there was just about enough space to teach everyone.

And what of the rest of the RCE during the war? The German occupation of Tournai in August 1914 cut off the French, English and American communities from the mother house and so Hillside was chosen by Rome as the place to establish an emergency novitiate. Despite the honour of this recognition, the extra fourteen postulants who entered during 1916 from Germany, Ireland, America, France and England made life at Sycamores somewhat cramped, though 'the postulants were happy to rough it and Mother Duchemin's unquenchable and motherly zeal created an atmosphere of gaiety and fervour that would have carried these novices through far greater hardships in their training for the religious life'.

The community at large were overjoyed to hear of Mother Duval's release from Tournai on Community Feast Day 1917, 100 years to the day since the founding of the Order. She was welcomed joyfully to Hillside in the spring of 1918, and on 4 May 1918 she received the vows of the first ten nuns of the RCE to make their profession in England.

Misty the donkey

Now Misty is a donkey and a lively one at that
He might be called good looking if he weren't quite so fat
To ride him seems quite easy, until you have a try
Then when you mount, up go his heels and on the ground you lie

In the winter term of 1918, the second form gave an entertainment called 'Mysteriosa' at which they sold things and had competitions. In this way they made several pounds with which to buy a donkey for the school to ride. In the beginning of March 1919 the donkey arrived, and the second class decided to call him Misty Eutrophelia. He was quite small with the cross on his back very well marked; he was five years old. When you went near him he would pretend to chase you, kicking all the while so that at first no one liked to venture too close to him. Then Ruth Hallinan, a girl in the second class, got a bridle sent to her from home, and having caught him gave us rides, not however without falls.

Below: Hillside from the air. The original house is on the left, the gym, hall and classrooms in the middle and the chapel on the right. Note the tennis courts and abundant woodland

The Hillside buildings were eventually returned to the community and it was decided to use them just for schooling, retaining The Sycamores as a home for the nuns and the boarders. The buildings were renovated and 'fitted out with all the requirements of an up-to-date school'. On 23 September 1921 it reopened under the name Hillside Convent College, and here the boarding and day schools were finally amalgamated under the headship of Mother Alma Mason. HCC was formally recognised by the Board of Education in December 1923.

Extracts from *The Hillside Magazine*, early twentieth century

This year, the Christmas play and concert was given in aid of the Belgian refugees. About a month before the fatal day there was a great hesitation as to whether there would be a play at all, as owing to Mother Dowling's illness and operation we had not had many rehearsals; however, we worked hard at it and when the day came *Twelfth Night* was voted a great success. The costumes were hired from London and were particularly nice. We regretted that we had not time to take any snapshots, but the day after we were all hurrying and scurrying in all directions – home for the Christmas holidays! Our fund reached approx £50 including the money raised by St Mary's for their concert, at which there was a tremendously large gathering.

The Easter Term is usually considered the dullest term of the school year. But this year, in spite of Lent and in spite of the war, we managed to pass it very enjoyably. It is known as the 'Concert Term' at Hillside, as each class generally favours the others with a concert.

Great was the consternation of all Hillsidians when the news spread one day that Madame Ramon, when crossing from St Mary's, had been knocked over by a motor car. Though ill for several weeks, she fortunately had no bones broken, but she had a very narrow escape. Madame Dowling, too, had a serious operation and spent the Easter term recuperating. She is now much better, we are glad to say.

We were favoured with several distinguished visits last term, first from our beloved bishop who is always so welcome at Hillside. On the day of his visit, the little ones caused much excitement by shutting up three of their little companions in the classroom cupboard, and for some minutes no one could open the door. His Lordship, on hearing it, was about to try his strength on the reluctant door when the news came that it was open. The prisoners were none the worse for their adventure, though perhaps a little wiser! Cupboards are now prohibited areas! The bishop on occasion of this visit added two extra days onto our Easter holiday; after this we loved him more than ever, if possible!

The Summer Term is unanimously voted as 'the nicest term of all'. Holidays are plentiful, tennis is in full swing and the greater part of the

Head girls.
From the top:
Cornelia Heffernan, the first head girl, 1927–8; Mary Roantree, 1929–30; Evelyn Pelly, 1930–1

day is spent out of doors. Night recreations also take place in the garden which is a great attraction, and hide and seek is a veritable craze. Photography too is the hobby of this term and we have taken some excellent snaps. On Whit Monday this year we had our annual picnic to the Empress's lake where we played cricket and hide and seek and some of us rehearsed our play for Reverend Mother's Feast. The time simply flew and we seemed to have been there no time before the signal was given for the return home.

The Feast of the Sacred Heart this year was awaited with expectant curiosity as to the intentions of Reverend Mother concerning the programme of our day. Should we, some pessimistic spirits demanded, be bound to worship at the feet of the muse of cube and square or repeat in smiling consistency the irregularity of 'cueillir' as the usual routine of the pursuance of studies demands? No, responded the optimists, certainly not, whoever heard of such a thing? We shall have a whole holiday! The actual fact, however, fell short of both conjectures... Father Conway chose the day as the most suitable occasion for distributing badges of the Apostleship of Study, and Reverend Mother of holding a grand garden party to which we were all invited. Of the former, little remains to be said. We were given the badges of the first and second degree, and left to wonder if we should ever attain to the sanctity of the sixth. The latter was somewhat of a novelty. The invited trooped down and arranged themselves in groups around the lawn. Then things began to go – in more sense than one! The guests were asked with what beverages they wished to stay their thirst and rejoined that they did not really mind as long as it was cold. As a result, sherbert was administered in mugs, patriotically ornamented with photos of Their Majesties the King and Queen of England and drunk with great gusto! The general conclusion was that Reverend Mother was a BRICK! The party wound up with tennis and thus the day came to a close.

Views of
The Sycamores,
1916–17, and *below*,
students, 1916

St Michael's Abbey

When Mesdames Murray Roantree and Desroullers arrived in Farnborough to plant the flag of the Religious of Christian Education at Hillside, St Michael's Abbey – or the Priory as it then was – gave an enthusiastic welcome to these pioneering nuns. The Priory was a great consolation to them. Its splendid church guaranteed them daily Mass and its lodge was their bed and breakfast till Hillside was habitable. The Sisters were amongst friends from day one. With the Empress Eugenie at the Hill and French canons at the Priory, they could want for nothing.

Today we think of the Abbey as a historic monument, but when the Sisters arrived it was all brand new. The bodies of Napoleon III and his son Louis had been installed just the year before and the Empress had not yet completed her first ten years at Farnborough Hill.

In 1895 the Norbertine Canons departed from Farnborough, and Benedictine monks from the Abbey of St Pierre de Solesmes took possession of the Priory. When the first three monks arrived to inspect the buildings, they made their way along the Farnborough Road to Hillside to introduce themselves to the Sisters. The monks rang the bell and pushed forward the one they thought to have the best English. He tried to explain himself, as best he could, until the nun who had answered the door finally responded in perfect French – her native tongue! The monks in turn celebrated Mass, each served by a boy, Edmund Fehrenbach, who joined them for the breakfast which followed. His name is remembered because this day made a profound impression on him: he later became a monk at the Abbey and three of his sisters were nuns at Farnborough Hill; after ordination in 1911, Dom Fehrenbach said his first Mass in the Hillside chapel. On that first meeting, encouraged by the warmth of the welcome, the monks accepted charge of the Abbey and in December 1895 five Benedictines arrived in Farnborough, living for some months in one of the Farnborough Hill lodges until the Priory was refurbished.

When the Sisters purchased the Empress's house, the relationship between school and Abbey was made even more concrete. Generations of girls ascending Farnborough Hill for the school day would see, through the trees, the dome of the

Abbey. It would inevitably be part of their memory for the rest of their lives. The monks continued to ensure daily Mass for the Sisters for the century which followed, and every celebration for more than a century was a celebration for the two communities, of the monks and the nuns. Feast days, professions, ordinations, jubilees would always see a contingent of one community supporting the other. Dom Cabrol, an internationally renowned liturgical scholar, would always find time to give spiritual conferences to 'his girls' at the Hill, many

of which are recorded in the school magazine. When the foundation stone of the fine new chapel was laid in 1931, it was Abbot Cabrol and the monks who led the ceremonies. The Abbot planted a cross where the high altar now stands, and climbed a scaffold to lay the foundation stone with the silver trowel which had been used for the same purpose at Hillside in 1893, and which is today preserved at the Abbey.

The monks looked forward to being on the rota for Mass at Farnborough Hill. Each monk had his own reason. For some it was the fresh air of the morning walk and the kindness of the girls and Sisters. For Abbot Cabrol it was the chance to smoke a cigar without arousing gossip among the monks and guests. For all the monks, the convent breakfast was legendary: the full cooked breakfast served to the priest in splendid solitude in the priests' parlour, and the linen, china and food, were a marked contrast to the monastery fare of dry bread and coffee!

When the Sisters took their official final bow from Lafosse House in October 2013, it was fitting that the Abbot of Farnborough and the monks of the Abbey should have supplied the ceremonies. Behind all the fine music, words and splendour of

St Michael's Abbey. *Top and below left*, views of the dome and interior; *above*, Empress Eugenie's tomb. Photographs taken by Farnborough Hill students

that day lay a hinterland unknown to most: more than a century of mutual support and friendship between the Benedictines of Farnborough and the Religious of Christian Education.

The monks have a happy daily reminder of this friendship. Every day a particular bell in the Abbey tower calls the monks to their midday prayer. It is the bell from Hillside Convent.
Abbot Cuthbert Brogan of St Michael's Abbey, Farnborough

'A nice social game of tennis': sport at Farnborough Hill

One of the earliest photographs taken of the schoolgirls of Hillside shows them demonstrating their skills at tennis and hockey, dressed in ankle-length skirts, high-necked, long-sleeved blouses and hats (see page 15). The clear message was that the school took sport seriously and included it in the curriculum. Hillside College eventually had quite extensive tennis and netball courts and a well-equipped gymnasium with wall bars and climbing ropes, and after the purchase of the Farnborough Hill estate the Sisters lost no time in establishing playing fields for the boarders.

At the time of writing, a century later, the PE department has four full-time teachers and some specialist coaches who are brought in on a part-time basis. They teach a range of sports, including netball, hockey, cricket, rounders, tennis, swimming, cross-country, badminton, athletics, basketball, dance, gymnastics and fitness, trampolining and more, and run a wide array of after-school activities on every school night of the week. In addition, they can average over 100 fixtures in a single term. They also run GCSE and A level courses in PE and organise regular sports tours and participate in many different district, county and occasionally national competitions. It is a far cry from the stated aim of the headmistress, Mother Rosemary Alexander, in the late 1960s that she wanted every girl to be able to play 'a nice social game of tennis' and to be able to swim.

The Hillside Magazine of 1924 lists ten 'net-ball' fixtures against such opponents as Chertsey and Basingstoke, while 'hockey has been played with energy during the winter terms, but we have not played any matches, reserving our main strength for net-ball'. In the summer, tennis was the only form of sport mentioned, but 'Reverend Mother is providing hard courts for us, so that we shall be able to practise in winter as well as in summer'. Revealingly, the anonymous author of the report began by stating, 'success or failure mean little to the true lover of games', thus demonstrating that she had not fully grasped the nature of sporting competition.

Opposite: Netball, 2010

Below: Tennis and hockey at Hillside before the First World War

Sister Bickford

Sport in the early 1930s was taught by Miss Bickford, who then left for a spell of teaching in Argentina before joining the Order and reappearing at her old school as Mother Bickford. Generations of Farnborough Hill girls remembered this formidable teacher sprinting across the hockey field with her habit pinned up at the front so she could move freely, waving a hockey stick in front of her to encourage the girls to run faster. She also taught Spanish and ran the secretarial course as well as acting as school bursar and dormitory mistress.

She could also be indulgent at times, as Nicky Hall (Turle) recalled: 'I started Spanish; being taught by her was pure delight. I would tell her – in Spanish, of course – that I had been to the farm (where Lafosse House now stands) over the weekend and milked a cow. This was most emphatically forbidden, but I knew she would treat this sort of information as "classified" and she always did... She was dormitory mistress of the red corridor and taught all sports (including frustrating attempts to teach me to dive into the frozen green swimming pool, and I would NOT do that, even for her!). She drove with considerable panache and would probably be caught for speeding these days.' Sister Bickford later became Reverend Mother and lived well into her nineties, retaining a sense of humour and her crisp way of speaking to the end of her days.

Greek dancing, 1930s

relay race and the 'ball race'. Meanwhile, for the browns, St Augustine's surged ahead of their deadly rival St Paul's, through such excitements as the 'slow bicycle race', the house tug-o'-war and the senior obstacle race.

Both blues and browns were able to use the gymnasium, which featured wall bars and a vaulting horse and allowed the girls to get exercise even when the weather was poor. Regaining their sports facilities had been one of the great benefits of having their buildings returned to them by the army in the summer of 1924. When the college was once more requisitioned in 1939, fifteen years later, the loss of the gymnasium was a considerable blow.

Sport was played in the normal school uniform, with a change of footwear the only concession to the activity; only 'Greek dancing' had its own costume – a long, flowing dress which enabled the wearer to move gracefully. Ballroom dancing was another popular 'extra' and, of course, was

In those days the school was strictly divided between the 'blues' and the 'browns', the boarders and the day girls, and all sports teams reflected this. Part of the reason lay with the fact that sport took place in the afternoon, when the day girls stayed in school while the boarders went to their home in the convent. The two groups played matches against each other, of course, underlining the (usually) friendly rivalry between the two groups. Once Farnborough Hill had been purchased in 1927, this division became even more marked as the distance between school and convent became so much greater.

Sports Days, in the 1920s as now, involved inter-house competition. However, the houses in those days were also either 'blue' or 'brown', so once again the two groups remained separate. The 'blue' house, St John's, won the Sports Cup in 1925, with spirited performances in both the

Gymnastics at Farnborough Hill:
In the Hillside gym, 1920s/30s ...

Swimming at Farnborough Hill: In the 1930s pool and in the same pool today minus the diving boards

performed in the usual uniform rather than the elegant gowns which no doubt the girls dreamed of one day owning. Indoor games lessons often started with girls marching around the gymnasium in order to check their posture and encourage graceful movement. 'Deportment' was taken seriously and listed alongside the hockey and netball results for each house. Good posture, walking gracefully and learning how to curtsey were considered social skills on a par with being able to dance. All girls were expected to curtsey to visitors (one foot behind the other and a quick bend of the knee) and they were also taught to make more elaborate deep curtseys on formal occasions. Gymnastics displays took place outside in the summer for the benefit of parents, and the houses competed against one another.

The really exciting sporting news of 1930 was the opening of a new 'swimming bath', realised through the

conversion of the building which was formerly the imperial museum. Although it was only 6ft 6in deep at the deep end it had three diving boards as well as a running springboard. It was heated, but it had no filtration system, so that as the term progressed the water became increasingly green; during the holidays the caretakers would empty, clean and refill it.

Then, as now, the school provided external speakers to provide coaching and inspiration; and there was also sometimes the opportunity to see professional games, either in Aldershot or further afield. Monica Shannon reported excitedly on the ladies' hockey match between England and Scotland in March 1933, won 2–1 by Scotland; fast forward to 2012 when an excited group of staff and girls attended the warm-up match for the Olympics featuring an old girl, Alex Danson, as a member of the bronze medal winning Great Britain women's hockey team. The same sense of excitement prevailed.

... in the old gym, 2002 ...

... and in the Mother Alexander Sports Hall, 2014

Right and far right: Lacrosse and tennis, 1953

Below: Netball, late 1930s

Below right: Hockey, 1970s–80s

Although netball was the dominant sport into the 1930s, by the end of the decade hockey was well established, with twenty matches listed against outside opponents and many more between houses. The outbreak of war, however, inevitably caused many disruptions, and not just to the hockey fixtures; one of the last formal sporting events to take place in the old gymnasium, before its loss to the army, was a gymnastics competition between the houses, blue and brown alike, in March 1939.

By 1941–2 two new sports supplemented the usual tennis, hockey and netball fixtures: lacrosse and rounders. Lacrosse continued as a regular school sport into the 1960s. Rounders, of course, remains part of the regular summer curriculum. Swimming, too, had become a competitive sport by this time with a modest fixture list. All these new sports were well established by 1943. Then in 1945–6, 'it was decided that we should play hockey during the Christmas term and lacrosse in the spring, so that by devoting one term to each game we should raise the standard.'

Gymnastics display, 1980s

In the late 1940s, when the system of blues and browns was abandoned in favour of the new green uniform, games kit was introduced in the same green colour: a green short skirt, thick green games knickers and airtex blouses. By the beginning of the 1950s, the PE curriculum was well established with three new games mistresses appointed. Tennis continued to be popular, and Jean Barrington, a boarder, was chosen to play for her county of Somerset in 1955. She reached the finals of the West of England junior singles and won the junior doubles. Meanwhile, the swimming pool finally had an effective heating system installed, and Scottish country dancing as a competitive activity also made an appearance. In 1960 table tennis was added to the competitive curriculum.

The 1960s may have been a time of radical social change, but until 1964 deportment colours continued to be awarded, for many years taught by Miss Peggy Dashper, who varied the instruction with lessons in the can-can. In 1965 the magazine's 'Games Notes' were co-written by a certain Ann Tristram, known to later generations of girls by her married name of Mrs Berry, who had been a natural all-rounder at school, excelling at a wide variety of sports. The report noted the last lacrosse match: 'the passing of "lax" from Farnborough was mourned by many, but it has been found that, with only a limited number of games lessons a week, it is impossible to teach all three winter games'.

After qualifying as a PE teacher in 1968, Ann Berry approached Mother Alexander for advice about which of two jobs she should choose. To her surprise, she was told to refuse both and return to her old school as a teacher. PE had become less popular over the years, with many older girls evading games lessons with a variety of ruses. Only a limited number of girls tried out for teams. A new approach was needed.

One of her early innovations was to reintroduce track and field sports to the curriculum, partly in an effort to include more girls in competitive sport. She also increased the number of teams in the traditional sports and, when the new gymnasium was built, brought in new events such as vaulting. And over the years more clubs were gradually introduced: aerobics, pop-mobility, table tennis, badminton, basketball and volleyball. Her career at the school took in six headmistresses in all, but she holds a special place in her heart for Mother Alexander, who had

such an important influence on her own life and career. It is in Mother Alexander's honour that the sports hall, which crowned Mrs Berry's time at the school, is named.

Mrs Berry was helped for much of her career by a former pupil, Jackie Ison (née Beill), who arrived at Farnborough Hill as a boarder in 1968. Jackie was another all-rounder, described as 'lively, friendly and extremely talented at sport; always to be found doing, not sitting'. She was in all the school teams and competed at a high level in swimming, diving, netball and gymnastics. After the Sixth Form, during which she was games captain, she went to Bedford College to study PE. After qualifying, she taught in Oxford and Croydon before returning to her old school where she

Ann Berry

Ann Berry's life has been intimately entwined with Farnborough Hill since the moment of her birth. Her mother had been a day pupil at Hillside and her grandfather had bought The Sycamores, formerly part of the school establishment, in the 1940s. It was here that Ann Tristram was born. She attended the school throughout her school career, and then returned after a three-year break training as a PE teacher. She spent the whole of her career at the school, serving both as head of PE and head of year.

Mrs Berry retired from teaching in 2007, after thirty-nine years continuous service. She remembers the 1980s as 'the golden years' with the Farnborough Hill gymnasts winning the National Schools Team Championship five times in six years (the off-year came when the district refused to pick them, evidently to give another school a chance). This was on top of a wide range of other competitive fixtures – a far cry from her original remit. Asked to sum up her time at Farnborough Hill, she said, 'I had thirty-nine wonderful years in a place which is deep in my heart. You could not wish for a better place to be. I loved it.'

Actress Juliet Aubrey, who was at the school in the 1980s, remembers Mrs Berry fondly: 'I had a teacher crush on her I think, and wanted to please her, to do my best, to score goals, left wing in hockey, goal attack in netball, and serve aces and thunder all down the baseline in tennis. She was so dedicated and enthusiastic. We were a good match for any school, and won fixture after fixture under her coaching and perseverance. I can see her dog and her car, parked up against the gymnasium wall. The clack clack of our hockey boots as we ran through the quad, and flew free as birds down the hill to the grass pitches.'

Left: Ann Berry (Tristram) in the 1960s

Below: Mrs Berry and the hockey team, 1980s

PE staff in the 1990s: left to right, Rosemarie Thompson, Jackie Ison (Beill) and Ann Berry (Tristram)

remained until her premature death in 2008. Her memorial service attracted generations of old girls who had played with and for her and who came to pay tribute to her dedication as a teacher. A cherry tree, planted in her memory, grows next to the path that leads down to the sports hall.

Upgrading the PE facilities took place at a modest pace. The Sisters were finally able to build a new gymnasium in 1965, as part of the St Joseph's complex. However, it could only accommodate one class at a time, so in wet weather they had to fall back on the school hall. Badminton and table tennis took place there into the new millennium and until the new sports hall was opened in 2005. Although the swimming pool had a new heating system, the changing rooms were dark and entry to the pool itself was via an unlovely brown foot-bath which many girls tried to step around. A proper filtration system was introduced in the 1970s, but updating the changing rooms had to wait until 2008.

Netball team, 1990s
with Alex Danson
front row, second
from left

Ninety-three separate hockey and netball fixtures were listed in the 1976–7 school magazine, in addition to six separate tournaments at district and county level. There were cross-country, basketball and athletics competitions and running, gymnastics and vaulting teams. Gymnastics, in particular, was starting to develop; the magazine gave a long list of girls who had gained British Amateur Gymnastic Association awards. By the early 1990s the 'Games' section of the school magazine had grown to six tightly packed pages, with reports and photographs of victorious teams in gymnastics, netball and even dressage.

In 1998 nine members of the Lower Sixth took the first sports leadership course. Practical and theory sessions during general studies gave the group skills in organisation and fitness. This can be seen as the precursor of the GCSE and A level courses in PE developed by the PE department during the following decade, which have proved very successful.

Alex Danson

Peering out from the front row of a junior netball squad in the school magazine of 1998 is Alex Danson. She came as a shy first year in 1996 and soon established herself as a talented sports player, rising quickly through the ranks of school, district, and county levels in her chosen field of hockey. By the time she came to study for her A levels she had her first international cap against Germany and later was part of the successful GB women's hockey team in the 2012 Olympics and 2014 Commonwealth Games, and their top scorer. Since leaving in 2003 she has returned to her old school several times to speak about her experiences and was a superb guest of honour at prize giving in 2011. This success was foreseen while she was at school by a classmate who wrote 'most likely to win an Olympic medal' in her school yearbook when she was doing her GCSEs.

I wasn't naughty but I would probably like to giggle or chat a lot in lessons. I missed a lot of school to play sport, especially as I got older. I spent every minute possible on a hockey pitch and would bribe anyone I could to come down to lunchtime practices. I had lovely friends I enjoyed spending my time with and remember spending far too much time in the tuck shop queue. I loved our inter-house competitions, Christmas quizzes and house fundraising projects – a cake sale or a raffle to help raise money for Becket House. I remember once doing a sponsored silence (that was hard!) and a sponsored ten-lap run around the double hockey pitches.

I have such fond memories of school for so many reasons, I loved that the day was full with activities. I attended everything and anything, from gym club to drama to recorder group as well as every sport going. School to me was a community where we were taught not only to try to do our best academically but that other things were of equal importance. Interacting with the community at harvest festival, having a strong

bond with all the nuns at Lafosse, celebrating other achievements inside and outside school are just a few examples. Farnborough Hill taught me to respect and be proud of being an individual, it allowed me to pursue my sporting dreams and both helped and encouraged me to do so. I feel so lucky that I had such a wonderful start, surrounded by staff, friends and a community of people that cared for me and for whom I also cared.

One of my happiest memories is winning the South of England netball tournament and going to the national finals with Mrs Ison and the team. Also hours and hours spent in the Sixth Form common room, laughing till we cried, playing endless pranks on each other and planning loads of exotic holidays we never went on! And there is a quote from Winston Churchill that I heard in an Assembly and have never forgotten: 'You make a living by what you get, but you make a life by what you give.'

Alex Danson

Alex displaying her Olympic bronze
medal with Sarah Buckle, 2012

Helene Raynsford

Helene Raynsford arrived at Farnborough Hill from the Royal Ballet School. An injury had put an end to a professional career as a dancer, and instead she concentrated on developing her academic studies and keeping fit through playing sport. In 2001, after she had left school, a head injury confined her to a wheelchair. She took up wheelchair basketball and was part of the GB team, winning two Paralympic Cup silver medals, before switching to rowing. The same determination which had carried her through earlier misfortunes helped her to win gold in the single sculls in the 2008 Paralympic Games in Beijing.

Left: The opening of the Mother Alexander Sports Hall in 2005. Anne Berry (Tristram) with Michael Maher, Chair of Governors, and, seated centre, Bishop Crispian Hollis

Below: Trampolining in the sports hall

Elizabeth Goddard, Helene Raynsford and Suzanne Hayes

2005 saw the long-awaited opening of the Mother Alexander Sports Hall, built on the site of a tennis/netball court at the foot of the hill. For the first time there was room to have several classes indoors at once, and scope for introducing new activities using trampolines and the fitness suite (with equipment donated by the Friends of Farnborough Hill). The old gym in the 1960s block up the hill was converted a few years later into a theatre. The old-fashioned wall bars and ropes were no longer needed as the emphasis in gymnastics had shifted to floor and vaulting routines. Meanwhile, the new dance studio in the St Joseph's Courtyard complex offered possibilities for dance and aerobics classes.

As part of her farewell to the school before her retirement in 2007, Mrs Berry organised a gym and dance display which took place in the school hall. Its inspiration lay in the large-scale displays for parents which she had organised and

taken part in many years before, but this time it embraced many forms of dance performed singly, in pairs and in groups, as well as the much-loved gymnastics routines. It proved so successful that it became an annual event in the school calendar, initially organised by sixth formers but now by the PE staff themselves. After that first evening, the venue changed to the sports hall, partly because it offered a bigger performance space and partly because the floor was less slippery. In its present guise it has become a popular event for parents and girls. Older girls help younger ones with their choreography encouraging participation in extra curricular gym and dance. It also fosters links with feeder schools who sometimes provide guest display teams.

There have been two highly successful sports tours to the West Indies in recent years. Parties of senior girls, accompanied by the PE staff, played hockey and netball while soaking up the April sunshine in Barbados and St Lucia.

To the delight of the girls, the games kit was redesigned a few years ago to reflect modern trends in both style and comfort. Out went the thick gym knickers to be replaced by 'skorts' (short skirts with integral shorts) and better track suits and tops with purple, white and green stripes. Mouth guards have also become compulsory for hockey in line with health and safety legislation.

The PE staff have continued to be great enthusiasts, encouraging girls to participate in many extra-curricular activities and compete in a vast range of after-school and weekend fixtures. Netball continues to dominate the autumn and winter programme, with over 100 matches in just one term played against other schools. One recent

innovation has been a 'sport for all' club on Fridays after school which offers trampolining, dance and gymnastics. As Faye Kelsey, Mrs Berry's successor as head of PE put it, 'Most key stage three sports are not "lifetime" ones; few girls carry on playing netball and hockey after they leave school. The three most likely to survive into adulthood are badminton, swimming and tennis. By including all three in the curriculum, girls are being encouraged to acquire the skills which will enable them to enjoy a lifetime of sporting activity. Encouragement by example is much more effective than lecturing.'

And what of the future? An all-weather astroturf pitch is in the planning stages, together with floodlighting to permit play after dark. It is a long time since the decorous young ladies of Hillside Convent College first posed with their wooden tennis rackets and old-style hockey sticks, but the role of the PE department in helping to 'educate the whole person' has not changed since the school's foundation.

Above: Barbados hockey and netball tour, 2009

Below: Today's games kit

2

The middle years

Above: Napoleon's 'N' features on many of the house's fixtures. This is on the door to the lower refectory which originally came from the Tuileries Palace

Up the Hill

Following the return to Hillside after the end of the First World War, the Sisters soon found that they had outgrown their old home. Even The Sycamores, which had been retained as a residence for the boarders and community, proved to be inadequate for the rapidly expanding numbers. Mother Roantree asked the community to join her in praying for guidance about whether to build on the gardens of their current home or to look for entirely new premises. Her prayers seem to have been answered when she heard, in 1926, that Farnborough Hill was to be sold following the unexpected death of Prince Victor Napoleon, Eugenie's heir. As the anonymous writer of *The Hillside Magazine*'s 'School Chronicle' puts it: 'a certain mysterious intention of the Reverend Mother's, for which we had long been praying, was now granted, and we should be able to leave this house which has now become too small… and should begin next term in the large and beautiful mansion that used to belong to the Empress Eugenie.' As a later architectural historian put it when describing the building, 'the work of an unsung rogue architect given unlimited resources, Farnborough Hill is an excellent example, in a rare state of preservation, of a rich Victorian's house in the country, with additional historical associations…'.

Empress and her ladies; the canopied locker-benches of carved walnut and the matching table which still stand in the entrance hall, bearing the signature of the sculptor, Carlo Canbri of Siena; two very large bookcases; the large dining room chairs in amber cut-velvet which are now ranged along the walls of the lower gallery; and all the fixtures including the crystal chandeliers.

Above: An engraving from the 1880 sales catalogue when Empress Eugenie bought the estate; and *left*, its cover and an inside page

Below: A table acquired from the Empress's estate

Mother Roantree's negotiations were successful, and over the summer the task of converting the imposing mansion into a suitable home for a substantial community of nuns and seventy boarders got underway. Most of the imperial possessions were either taken back to the continent by Prince Victor's widow or sold at auction, but only a few of the larger pieces were within the community's financial reach. Among these were the pitch-pine altar and prie-dieu of the little chapel at the top of the building which Eugenie had established; the picture of Our Lord and the disciples at Emmaus which now hangs in the front hall in the place of the famous Winterhalter painting of the

Top: A detail from the table

Right: One of the canopied locker benches, and *above*, a detail of the armrest

Left: One of the Empress's chandeliers still in the lower refectory

Above: *The Supper at Emmaus* on the wall above the Empress's table

Opposite: The amber-cut velvet chairs in the lower gallery

In addition, Mother Roantree was able to buy the famous Agra carpet that fitted the lower gallery for what seemed at the time the staggering sum of £100. She is supposed to have consulted the Rector of Beaumont, Father Aston Chichester, SJ, who reassured her that, provided it would last twenty years, a sum of £5 per year on carpets would hardly infringe her vow of poverty, as she had feared. The carpet, especially made for the lower gallery by prisoners in Agra, was 'cream-coloured with a delicate design in blue and red', comparable to one ordered by Queen Victoria for Windsor Castle at the same time. No doubt worried about the effect of so many feet on so valuable a carpet, the community developed the habit of rolling it up and storing it under the stairs except when important visitors were expected. Unfortunately, this practice enabled moths to attack it unnoticed, and it

eventually had to be discarded. The floor has been kept bare ever since.

As Mother Mostyn records in *The Story of a House*, 'Almost immediately after the summer term ended, three or four of the nuns were sent to Farnborough Hill in order to place the furniture that was brought over from The Sycamores. For the time being they were allowed to sleep in any room they liked, each one being provided with a mattress but no bedstead. So two of them chose the highest point in Farnborough, the central tower with its magnificent views of the country on every side.' Having to descend ninety steps to answer the front door soon made the disadvantages of such a headquarters apparent, and the room was eventually given over to be a bedroom for novices who were presumed young and active enough to cope with the stairs.

Eventually the larger bedrooms, including the Empress's bedroom, became dormitories for juniors and seniors, while the Prince's Room became a common room and study. Mother Roantree used the Queen of Spain's room and other members of the community were dispersed around the smaller rooms or slept behind screens in the dormitories if they were in charge.

The heart of any community is its chapel, and one of the first alterations to be made that summer was the conversion of what had been two separate rooms into a large and elegant space for communal worship at the south end of the house. Now the school library, this new chapel was fitted out with pews brought from The Sycamores. When the school chapel was built in the 1930s, the temporary school library became a communal living room for the Sisters, and later still a music room, now called M1.

While these alterations were going on, the Sisters were able to use the Empress's chapel in what is now IT1. This had windows looking out towards the Abbey and had allowed Eugenie to see the spot where her husband and son were buried. Abbot Cabrol from the Abbey arranged for them to have daily Mass, even as they worked to make the place habitable.

Mother Mary Dawson Murray made several trips to London to buy oak bedsteads, wardrobes and washstands specially made for the large new dormitories. These supplemented the items they were able to buy locally and allowed the place to look fairly furnished, though Sister Rennie, who came as a boarder nine years later, remembers a Spartan atmosphere in the dormitories even then: uncurtained windows and rows of beds along the walls on bare floorboards with just a strip of carpet down the centre of the room. The same conditions prevailed in the novices'

Left: The sick bay, now known as St Luke's

Below: The dormitory in the Empress's bedroom, later to become the present-day Sixth Form common room

room at the top of the tower as late as the 1940s. Sister Wright remembers being puzzled during her first night there by a strange light moving across the wall, before realising that it was the reflection of a passing train.

Providing bathing facilities for so many people was another challenge that summer. More bathrooms had to be installed along with a proper hot water system. The few existing baths had each had their own gas-fired geyser; Sister McDonnell remembers one of these 'geyser rooms' on the top floor of the main house as late as the 1960s. Even with new facilities, there always had to be rotas for baths, which were limited to three nights a week for boarders; girls queued for their turn, hoping that the hot water would hold out. For ordinary washing, each girl had a jug and basin on a wash stand near her bed, with the 'slops' being emptied in a nearby large sink. Although the building did have some central heating, the large bare windows and high ceilings ensured that the dormitories were often very cold in winter. The novices' room had no heating at all, and it was not uncommon to find that the water in the jugs had frozen solid in the night.

Outside, the statues of Our Lady of the Sacred Heart and St Joseph, which had stood in the grounds of Hillside, were installed, and tennis courts were set out on the hilltop beyond the house on the spot where the chapel was later to be built. At the foot of the hill, where they remain to this day, hockey pitches were marked out. The glass-roofed quad was equipped to become a changing room and also doubled as an indoor recreation area for the boarders, where they could play volley ball or sardines among the lockers.

A palpable air of excitement shines in the usually sober prose of the magazine that summer, as community and boarders contemplated the move to their new home. After it was officially announced, 'excitement ran high all the term whenever Farnborough Hill was mentioned. Our first visit to it, after this announcement, was on Whit Monday. A picnic had been planned to take place in the grounds of the newly acquired mansion, but the morning was so wet that this project had to be abandoned, and we contented ourselves with exploring the park and shrubberies, lawns and kitchen garden during the afternoon, returning to Hillside for tea on the veranda.' The same excitement is evident in the account of the new school year: 'On 28 September, Farnborough Hill opened its great doors to the eighty-nine girls who were to make it their school. No need to dwell on the excitement and pleasure experienced in visiting all its rooms and in trying to acquaint ourselves with its somewhat intricate geography… The next day, being Michaelmas Day, a crocodile of chattering maidens wended its way to the Abbey to assist at Pontifical High Mass, and to celebrate the joyful event of Abbot Cabrol's golden jubilee, feeling that this was a fitting start for the new school year…

The first Sunday of the term saw us all assembled in the red (now called the green) gallery since the blessing of the temporary chapel had not yet taken place. The following day the bishop… blessed the chapel with full pomp and ceremony, and said the first Mass in it… Now school life was in full swing. We had found on our arrival that everything was ready for us; nothing had been forgotten. Our netball courts were marked out, and a practising ground for hockey prepared, while the making of a full-sized hockey field was in progress, so that we have been able to start our games and practise for future matches.'

Farnborough Hill provided the community and the boarders with much larger premises, and as they settled in further alterations, additions and use of the space suggested themselves. End of year speech day entertainments and other plays could be held out of doors on what became known as the 'Hiawatha Lawn', named after the dramatic rendering of Longfellow's poem first performed there in 1933 and repeated several times since. Nativity and Passion plays, however, needed to take place indoors and so temporary stages were erected in the lower gallery, with the orchestra providing the music from the grand salon and

Hockey and – pictured here – cricket are played on the field below the house

The local area

The advertisements placed in *The Hillside Magazine* by local businesses in the 1930s give some sense of what Farnborough itself was like. The main road outside the school was still a country lane, though the area near the railway station was busier. The Farnborough and Aldershot Riding Establishment boasted 'terms very moderate. We undertake to teach you all about horses and horsemanship. Horses and ponies supplied and tuition given to the pupils of Hillside Convent.' Silcock's Poultry Foods full page advertisement again hinted at a largely rural community. WM Rowe and Co Ltd, 'manufacturers of juvenile clothes and outfitting', were the school's official tailors and outfitters despite being inconveniently located down in

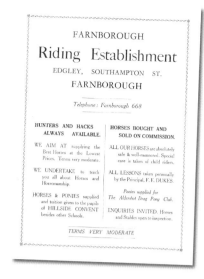

An advertisement for a local business, 1930s; and *right*, an illustration from the school magazine, *c* 1930

Gosport. Perhaps not surprisingly, there were quite a few suppliers of 'devotional requisites', including the Benada Abbey Lace School in County Sligo, Ireland ('orders earnestly requested to enable us to give employment to our poor girls'). The Tumble Down Dick Hotel was evidently in its heyday, to judge by the photograph of a handsome, ivy-clad facade with elegant open-topped cars parked outside, and 'excellent cuisine' within.

'noises off' coming from the Oak Parlour (later the headmistress's office). Sunday evening lantern lectures were held upstairs on the green gallery. A particularly memorable one was recalled some years later by a past pupil in *The Hillside Magazine*. The boarders were told that 'a certain Professor Taille of the Sorbonne was coming to give us a lantern lecture that evening, and accordingly all assembled in the green gallery and some helped to put up the lantern. The professor arrived, and by the dim light we judged her to be a somewhat frumpy university woman of uncertain age.

It was a relief to find that she was prepared to lecture in English, on Napoleon, and we stoically kept our countenance, remembering our good manners, even when the lecturer's broken English struck us as comic. But we were not prepared for her to take off her hat, after the last slide had been shown, and reveal the well known features of one of the sixth formers, Ena Tighe. Our "professor" received an ovation, and if the other lantern lectures of the term all proved instructive, this one at least may claim to be the best remembered.'

Left: The Oak Parlour

Above: The library, now M1

Below and bottom left:
The Grand Salon, with its
infinity mirrors, *right*

Bottom right: The painted
ceiling of the Empress's
dining room

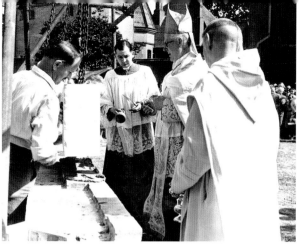

Far left: The chapel during construction, 1932

Left: The blessing of the foundation stone, 1931

Below: The consecration of the chapel, 1932, showing nuns seated along the sides, girls in white veils, as was traditional then, and the temporary altar at the front

Meals at Farnborough Hill were at first taken by the boarders and community in the Empress's elegant dining room, underneath the painted ceiling and crystal chandeliers. As the school continued to grow, Mother Roantree decided to add an additional dining area, with sleeping accommodation above to act as a bridge to the elegant, purpose-built chapel she had dreamed of since the community's arrival at Farnborough Hill. She called in the prominent architect, Adrian Gilbert Scott, who had made a speciality of building churches and had worked with his brother, Sir Giles, on the designs for Liverpool's Anglican Cathedral. Incidentally, so successful was this first commission that Adrian Gilbert Scott remained responsible for all the school's additions until 1962, a year before his death.

The chapel he designed would hold more than 500 people and is still able to accommodate the much larger school that exists today, more than eighty years later. Fundraising commenced at the end of the 1920s, and with a significant sum already raised, the first sod for the new wing was cut on the feast day of St Joseph, 19 March 1931. In addition to the extended dining hall, there was to be a cloister running alongside which provided a covered alternative route to the new chapel and led onto the lawns. When the wing was finished, the foundation stone of the new chapel was laid on 21 November, Community Feast Day, in a ceremony presided over by Abbot Cabrol in place of the bishop, after which the new refectory was put to good use with a tea for guests, students, parents and community. The magazine noted the new 'sturdy tables of silvered oak, to match the panelling'. It is a tribute to the workmanship of the original craftsmen, not to mention the care of subsequent generations of kitchen helpers and of the girls who used them, that these same tables are in daily use eighty years later, and are still in good condition.

Money continued to flow into the chapel fund and work went on apace such that, exactly a year after its foundation stone was laid, on 21 November 1932, the new chapel was opened. The day was unseasonably bright and sunny so that the students, community and guests saw 'brilliant

sunshine streaming into the sanctuary through the tall hidden windows at the moment of the consecration'. The altar, however, was a temporary one, and it was not until 3 October 1934 that the high altar which had been part of the original design was completed and consecrated with another ceremony, to coincide with Mother Roantree's golden jubilee of profession. The pews were the gift of the old girls, who also contributed to the organ, known as 'Bertha', which was not installed until after the war.

William Johns

William Johns, whose efforts to keep the girls fed in their unexpectedly prolonged stay at St Bernadette's were so appreciated, was the school caretaker, chauffeur and general handyman for forty years. He arrived as a garden boy in 1918, working under his father and uncles, and quickly made himself indispensable to the Sisters with his 'genial smile and genuine helpfulness', not to speak of his willingness to turn his hand to almost anything which needed doing. He lived in the chauffeur's lodge, then called Mary's Meadow (now Mary Meadow Cottage) and became a permanent member of the school community, seldom taking his full annual holiday so that he could allow the Sisters a rest in the kitchens over the summer. When he died unexpectedly in 1958, such was his popularity that one observer remarked that his funeral might have been that of a prince, so impressive was the cortege and the number of mourners.

Above: A group at Bexhill-on-Sea, late 1930s

Above left: Mother Mary Dawson Murray on the beach at Climping, supervising the girls on a seaside outing

A further exciting new facility for the boarders was announced in *The Hillside Magazine* of 1936–7: a holiday house in Bexhill-on-Sea. As the magazine explains, 'The number of children whose parents, residing in the Dominions or elsewhere at a distance, are obliged to leave them at Farnborough Hill for the holidays has made it necessary for us to take a house at the seaside summer after summer. This year, Reverend Mother has seized upon a favourable opportunity of buying a house at Bexhill-on-Sea, to which we can now repair and take the children whenever a change of air is needed.'

The house, overlooking the sea and equipped with a garden and tennis courts, was dedicated to St Bernadette. The first party of girls to visit, shortly after the purchase, endured a difficult journey which had made them arrive 'two hours later than they were expected, the driver having lost his way and taken them round a large slice of the south coast. Reverend Mother had the beautiful idea of keeping them all for the night, or their stay would have been too short. They bivouacked in the then half-furnished rooms, some sleeping on the beds, others on the floor with blankets kindly lent by the Reverend Mother of Nazareth House…. William (the school caretaker and handyman, who had come along) hastily went out into the town to produce extra provisions and his catering and cooking were greatly appreciated….' After this dramatic start, St Bernadette's became a comfortable holiday home for both boarders and community.

Many of the boarders had parents in the Diplomatic Service or in senior positions in the armed services and those who were able to visit them sent back accounts of trips to a surprisingly wide variety of destinations. 'Mes Premieres Impressions sur Paris' by Irene Groocock (pictured above, standing far left) in 1937 is supplemented by 'A Letter from Elsie Rickman' describing a trip to Algiers and Rome, 'The Call of India' by Stella Eardley-Wilmot and 'Chinese Adventures' by Violet Moore.

St Bernadette's was left unused during the war. Its position on the south coast made it vulnerable to the threat of invasion and in any case wartime petrol rationing and travel restrictions made visits impracticable. After the war, the need to look after boarders during the summer months no longer existed and it was sold.

Left: Reverend Mother Roantree with the Duke of Alba and Berwick (the Empress's nephew) at the 1939 opening of the Jubilee Wing and garden fete

Inset: The new wing shortly after completion – the hall and classrooms taken from the Hollybush Lawn

One final major building project was undertaken at the end of the decade. The occasion was the golden jubilee of the school in Farnborough and it was marked by the construction of a new assembly hall with classrooms and what would eventually become senior bedrooms above it.

The foundation stone was laid by the Spanish ambassador in May 1939, and the builders obviously worked hard at their task because the new wing was essentially finished by the time war was declared in September of that year and Hillside was once more requisitioned.

The Jubilee Wing in 2014

Above: The school, 1939

Right: Parents' Day, summer, late 1920s or early 1930s, taken at Farnborough Hill, with Mother Fehrenbach on the right

School days

What was it like being a schoolgirl at Farnborough Hill and Hillside during the inter-war period? Between the official accounts of buildings opened and Masses sung lie countless hours of daily life and education.

Until the summer of 1939 Hillside remained the main teaching establishment, so the boarders' day would begin early with a rising bell about 7am. They had twenty minutes to wash, dress and hurry downstairs for morning prayers before breakfast, which had to be taken in silence. Then they hurried back upstairs for a few minutes to collect their books and make their beds, before they set out, escorted by the younger teachers, to walk the one and a quarter miles from Farnborough Hill to Hillside. A new white cob, Polly, was bought to pull a cart piled high with their school bags and also give a lift to some of the older teachers who found the long walk a strain. When they arrived the girls joined the day girls in a 'hut' which acted as a locker and recreation room, where they could hang up their coats and change into indoor shoes. The day girls, of course, lived locally, and made their own way to school on foot or by bicycle, but both sets of girls had to be ready to march into Assembly at 8.45, often played in, in the 1930s, by a talented pair of musical sisters, Pat and Jo Keane.

Rather than repeat the process for afternoon school, the boarders and day girls pursued separate activities, with the day girls remaining at Hillside and the boarders having sport in the grounds or handicrafts and cookery lessons in their new home. This reinforced the clear distinction between the two groups of girls, known as the 'blues' and the 'browns' in reference to their separate uniforms. Mary Rose Murphy, a day girl (brown) in the 1930s, remembers that the two groups were not encouraged to mix, and sat on different sides of the classrooms. House activities also took place in the afternoons and for this reason the houses too remained quite separate, with different sports teams and other activities.

Audrey Baker, writing in the centenary edition of *The Hillside Magazine*, has vivid memories of those days: 'In the summer term our uniform was a choice of pale green, yellow or pale mauve cotton dresses, green shoes and a straw hat – we looked very colourful against the black habits of the nuns! In the winter it was said that the residents of Farnborough used to set their clocks by the crocodile of red berets and green overcoats as we walked to the college – so precise was our timing. Our winter uniform was a very smart V-necked navy blue gym tunic, cream blouse and school tie with the same green jersey as today. After games we changed into a navy blue skirt, blouse and tie at teatime. For daily morning Assembly at the college we lined up in forms, juniors at the front, for prayers and announcements, and then marched out to piano music. Each girl as she turned to leave the hall bowed to Reverend Mother who, with the community and staff, was on the dais. At all other times when we met or passed Reverend Mother a curtsey was made.'

Mornings were given over to academic studies, including then, as now, history, French, religious knowledge, English, geography, arithmetic, science and, for the older girls, German, physics, chemistry and biology. French seems to have been especially emphasised since the Abbot, a regular visitor, always gave his sermons in French and was evidently understood by most of his hearers. At 12.30 morning school ended and the boarders returned to Farnborough Hill for lunch, while day girls either went home, if they lived close enough, or had their lunch at Hillside. Afternoon school began at 2pm and day girls and boarders pursued similar, though separate programmes: sports, arts, music and handicrafts, either at Hillside or Farnborough Hill.

Above: Sixth Form with Miss Knight in the garden at Hillside, 1938

Below: Dining room at The Sycamores, *c* 1914–27

A shorthand and typing class in the 1950s, possibly with Sister May Shannon

Sister Rennie, a boarder who came to the school in 1935, remembers that on weekdays tea would be at 4pm, followed by evening prayers and study. Supper was at 7pm, and then they had half an hour's recreation. For juniors this took place in the quad, while older girls practised ballroom dancing, played the piano or listened to gramophones in the 'Hut', an old wooden prefabricated building which had been transplanted from its previous location in The Sycamores and was much prized by the girls as their own private recreation space. Bedtime was 9pm. Saturday afternoons often involved a sporting fixture against another school and on Sunday, after Mass in the chapel and dinner, there was sometimes a magic lantern show or conjurer, or other entertainment. Quite often, however, the girls were expected to amuse themselves and sometimes put on plays for one another, often organised by the houses.

The roll of prizes in the 1935–6 magazine lists 'day students' and 'resident students' separately and records commendations for 'examination work, with special mention' in mathematics, botany, French, physics, needlework, geography and arts and crafts for girls in the Upper V and VI, while lower down the school, class II gained recognition for Bible history, needlework and catechism as well as reading and spelling. The Lower V also had a 'secretarial form' who learned shorthand (theory and practice), typewriting and needlework.

Thanks ever so much for the lovely long letter you sent. I hope you are enjoying yourself in Switzerland. I am having quite good fun here at school. I expect I told you that I am now in domestic science. Compared to the other class we don't do a spot of work, but I seem to have learnt many more things than before. Every Wednesday and Thursday we cook our own lunches and we are allowed to make what we like which is jolly nice. We all work in pairs and I do my cooking with Jean. I also have first aid lessons which are very interesting. This morning we learnt how to make bandages and slings. I have also learnt all about shock and things like that and what to do when you find someone unconscious in the middle of the road (which is very unlikely). One part of the domestic science wing is turned into a modern flat and this we take in turns to sweep and dust etc. You have to be very careful because the mistress goes round afterwards and pushes her fingers along everything to see if there is no dust left.

Most of the school have suddenly developed flu and the infirmary is so full that they had to use a dormitory as well. Lots of my friends caught it but so far I am safe, thank goodness. One girl even developed chickenpox but she has been isolated.

On Shrove Tuesday we are having the famous annual fancy dress ball. This time we have all got to go as either a character or a title of a book. I am going to carry a candle upside down and to put my hair in curlers. I expect I'll look an awful sight but I don't care. I don't know what anyone else is going as, as they are all keeping it a very dark secret.

They are building a lovely new concert hall which I hope will be finished by next Speech Day as this year is the school's jubilee year and we must have something grand to celebrate it. But the point is that there are a lot of workmen floating round the grounds and at the beginning of the term, the headmistress, Mother Horan, told us that we were not to go anywhere near them, that we were strictly forbidden to speak to them. In fact, they won't let us go down to the games courts the way we usually go as it passes the place where they are building the new hall. Don't you think it silly? I do hope you are coming to England before going back to Tangier. Tons of love, Joey

Josie (Joey) Silva, writing in the school year 1938–9

Sodality: Children of Mary in their white dresses and blue cloaks, taken on the feast of Corpus Christi

The many prizes associated with religion are a reminder of the nature of the school, with nuns making up most of the teaching staff as well as providing the administrative and domestic support for the boarders. Almost all the boarders and many of the day girls were practising Roman Catholics, and religious faith was central to the life of the school. Indeed, the chapel at Hillside acted as a parish church for the wider Catholic community for a number of years before a purpose-built church was opened nearby. Sodalities played an important part in strengthening the faith of boarders, who wore different-coloured ribbons to denote their membership of the different groups.

Punishments were mild by the standards of the time. Mary Rose Murphy recalls that one of the worst was having a note sent home to your parents. However, the sharp tongues of some of the teachers ensured that this was seldom necessary. In addition there was a system of house points. Each girl began the school year with 100 points and had them deducted over the course of the year for infringements such as poor posture or running in the corridors. No one ever managed to retain all 100 points.

School reports, by modern standards, seem terse, often with single-word comments like 'fair' together with a sometimes devastatingly candid summing up at the end: 'Madeline appears not to have applied herself this year, being too much taken up with sport.' The girls were equally devastating in their comments about some of their teachers. Miss Murphy remembers one English teacher being known behind her back as 'the wild man of Borneo'. Others, however, remember the dedicated women, and occasionally men, who taught them much more fondly.

The Hillside Magazine of 1937–8 mentioned an innovation: 'A new and complete course of domestic science is projected and will be opened in September, in the house adjoining the college. The curriculum will include both a finishing course in homecraft and a preparatory course for those intending to enter a training college for domestic science.' Although to modern readers this looks like a retrograde step, lowering the sights of girls from academic careers to the roles of being good wives and mothers, in fact it throws an interesting light on the social upheavals which had been taking place in British society since the war. In an earlier era, the girls who went to Hillside and Farnborough Hill would not have expected to do their own cooking and cleaning, but instead would have employed domestic help to carry out the household chores. In this modern world, girls would increasingly have to manage for themselves, and elevating these tasks to a 'science' was proclaiming them to be worthy uses of a woman's time with skills that could be mastered by instruction rather than simply absorbed by practice.

Barbara Howells' (Zamoyska) school report, 1949

HILLSIDE CONVENT COLLEGE
FARNBOROUGH HILL, HAMPSHIRE

Term ending...........July.............1949

Barbara Zamoyska.................... Form....Lower VI.... Number in Form......19....

SUBJECT	Percentage	Position	Number Exam'd	REMARKS	SIGNATURE
Christian Doctrine	69	3	20	Very good work.	A.Horne RCF
Scripture					
Church History				Good but spoils work by 'rushing' it.	H. James RFC
English	42	1	6		
History					
Geography					
French					
German					
Latin, Div.				Has improved this term, but she often makes great mistakes in grammar.	M. Michalajuski
Greek Polish	64	1	2		
Arithmetic, Div.					E.S.G.Kendall IH.Ba..
MATHEMATICS Algebra, Div.				Good.	
Geometry, Div.					A.J.Donald A.P., B.Sc
Nature Study				Satisfactory	N.B.Dixon
Biology	60	2	4	Can do good work but must make much more effort.	E.S.G.Kendall IH.Ba..
Chemistry	47	1	4	Very good.	
Physics	68	2	5		
Art					
Needlework					
Elocution				Has considerable talent and has done very good work.	Elisan GPen
Pianoforte					
Singing					
Violin				Did very good work.	H.Smith

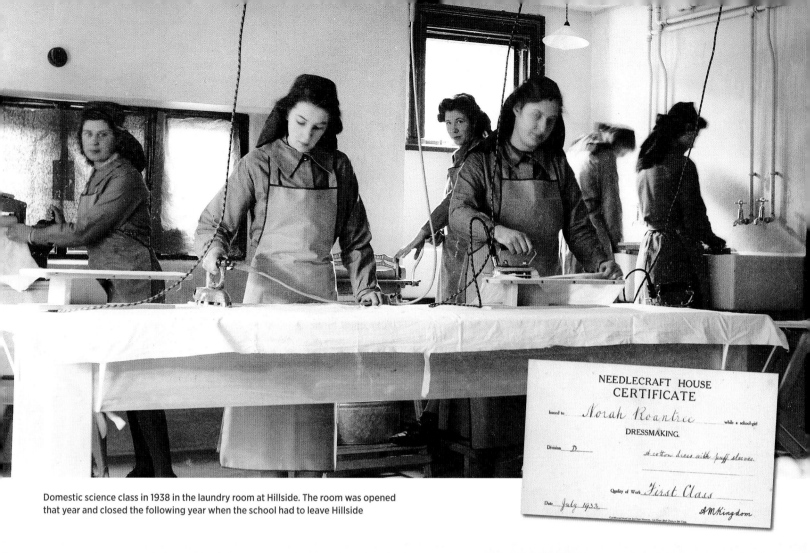

NEEDLECRAFT HOUSE
CERTIFICATE

Issued to *Norah Roantree* while a school-girl

DRESSMAKING.

Division **D** *A cotton dress with puff sleeves.*

Quality of Work *First Class*

Date *July 1933* *AMKingdom*

Domestic science class in 1938 in the laundry room at Hillside. The room was opened that year and closed the following year when the school had to leave Hillside

I started at Hillside in 1928 aged seven, as a day girl, and was warmly welcomed by Mother Mattes. In those days, while Catholics had a specific class for religious instruction and prayers, non-Catholics had a free period which was given over to embroidery, and sewing. In my first year I somehow managed to join this group (unintentionally) and even finished a cross-stitch purse before my mother found out that I was not getting the religious instruction for which I had been sent to the convent!

Mother Roantree was the Reverend Mother and I remember Mother Susan Shannon, Mother Justina, Mother Fehrenbach for music, Mother Mostyn and Mother Bickford. Among the lay teachers there were Miss Bourne (English), Miss Coles (biology), Mrs Austen for maths and Miss Gritton for singing and music.

School summers of course were always longer and hotter than those of today, and we always seemed to be lucky with the weather when staging events. I remember a dance programme on the lawn at Hillside, a production of 'Hiawatha' at Farnborough Hill, also on the lawn, and a production of *The Pirates of Penzance*, where I played the part of Frederick, although I think this was indoors and probably a Fifth or Sixth Form performance. My favourites were always the Christmas Carol concert, and trips to Woking for school choir and solos competitions – we went by train, which for me was as exciting as the singing. I can also remember going to Farnborough Hill for the annual retreats – there were a couple of trees in the grounds which could provide above ground seats for reading and avoiding notice!

I still have my St Joan of Arc house captain's badge, and my Child of Mary medal, although the ribbon unfortunately disintegrated in the

tropics. I loved gym and games and recall that the boat race was much more of an event than it is these days, and we always had Oxford and Cambridge netball matches, the teams wearing dark and pale blue.

I should have left school in 1939 to go on to the London School of Economics, but with the outbreak of war my mother decided against this and I came back to Hillside to do the secretarial course run by Mother Bickford. This took place up in the attics, which disguised the noise of the typewriters! By this time I was driving my own car to school, which I was allowed to park in the quad.

I remember my school days with great affection. They were happy years and I hope that present day pupils will have the same feelings.
Maureen Webber (Wright)

'Educating the whole person' has always been the school's philosophy and this is evident from the school's earliest days in the accounts of sports fixtures, concerts, plays and school holidays (often, as in the Shrove Tuesday fancy dress ball, literally associated with holy days). The boarding school had a large number of girls of Irish descent and St Patrick's Day, 17 March, was always celebrated with a holiday from lessons and a spirited England v Ireland hockey match.

All Saints Day was preceded by Halloween-like celebrations the night before, and the Feast of Corpus Christi saw elaborate processions all around the grounds of Farnborough Hill. These processions, which lasted until the end of boarding, saw the girls setting up altars in the grounds and strewing them and the pathways with blossoms from the rhododendron bushes. As part of their uniform, girls needed a white dress and white veil to be worn on this and other formal occasions, and in their snowy dresses and accompanied by a band from Sandhurst Military Academy, they followed the procession of priests around from altar to altar.

The 1933 performance of 'Hiawatha' on the lawn facing the Farnborough Road was the first of many dramatic performances which were put on for the benefit of parents and guests who had come for the school's annual prize day in the summer term. Photographs of these events show lines of girls in 'Greek dance' tunics or performing gymnastics routines. Plays and musicals were performed (Gilbert and Sullivan operettas were particular favourites) and the choir and orchestra gave special concerts as well as providing the music for services in the chapel. Art and literature were also encouraged; the Literary Society seems

Corpus Christi processions

to have been especially active, though the secretary admits in 1937 that they had suspended their meetings for a time in order to listen to 'a series of talks on Shakespeare (which) was running on the wireless at the time at which we usually held them. Those who were interested foregathered and listened in – we were especially intrigued by the different points of view put forward by Mr Val Gielgud and Mr Alfred Hitchcock.'

No school, not even a boarding one, can exist in a bubble, cut off from the outside world. *The Hillside Magazine* for 1935–6 opened with a reflection on recent national events: 'On the almost unclouded rejoicings of last year [the celebrations of the King's silver jubilee] has followed the national and world-wide grief in which Hillside had its full share – the death of our beloved King, George V, for whose soul our prayers have gone up to heaven, as also for Queen Mary and King Edward VIII. God prosper him!' The following year, as the magazine recorded, 'All this week the country was in suspense over the constitutional crisis and we were grieved to hear on

The fancy dress party

The fancy dress party took place in the Hut on the evening of Shrove Tuesday. We had a half holiday, so there was no homework that evening and no games in the afternoon as it was given up entirely to finishing our dresses. Directly luncheon was over, we all went upstairs to our dormitories or rooms and continued the making of our paper dresses. After about ten minutes our dormitory was strewn with every kind and colour of crepe paper, cardboard and drawing paper – not to mention tubes of sticky-paste, reels of cotton and all kinds of odds and ends. The dresses had to be our own original idea, and we had to do the making ourselves as well. There were, of course, exceptions to this among the small ones, who were allowed to be helped by the bigger girls or their dormitory mistresses.

At about half past four the tea bell rang, and we all trooped downstairs. If we had finished before it was time, we were allowed to go up again and give our dresses their finishing touches, as there were no prayers. That done, we could go down to the Hut and get ready for the parade.

Then Reverend Mother and Father Mangan came in, and the parade round the Hut began. First came the couples. They marched up to where Reverend Mother and Father Mangan sat, bowed or courtesied [*sic*] according to their gender and then walked down the side, in line. After the couples came the single girls. They did the same thing as the couples. Then, when the parade was over, the dancing began. It was great fun!

After we had danced for nearly an hour, and were all thoroughly exhausted, Mother Horan gave out the juniors' prizes. That was very exciting! The first prize went to Mickey and Minnie Mouse... and the senior first prize went to the Horse.... The staff came in and danced as well and I think they enjoyed it as much as we did.

Vivien Chapman, writing in The Hillside Magazine *of 1935–6*

Above: Sixth Form with Mother Horan, taken in 1938. The girl third from the left at the front is Sister Rennie's sister Mary

Above right: Prefects' common room, Hillside, 1920s

Right: The Marquis Room, which was a prefects' study, taken between 1927 and 1939, after which it became a dormitory. It is now the RE office

Thursday, the 10th, the proclamation of the abdication of King Edward VIII. We were allowed to listen in to Mr Baldwin's speech, and on Friday the seniors heard the now Duke of Windsor's speech over the wireless.' And then the 'rumours of war' in the Christmas term of 1938 became more noticeable: 'We spent the evening of 27 September being fitted with gas masks while the first black-out of our lives took place on the evening of the 28th, intensifying the mingled feelings of excitement and awe inspired by that memorable last week of September. We formed a "chain of prayer" for peace, lasting throughout the vital day of Mr Chamberlain's visit to Hitler, and when next morning at breakfast we were told of the Prime Minister's success we decided to spend the day in thanksgiving.'

In May 1939 a grand celebration was held in honour of the school's golden jubilee in Farnborough. But war loomed. The editorial in *The Hillside Magazine*, written in September after its outbreak, refers rather ruefully to the

fact that events had overtaken both the publication itself and the entire school: 'The magazine's apology for its late appearance is based partly on the fact that it had been planned in ample proportions, which required more than the usual time to edit… and partly on the subsequent disturbances of the autumn…. Our more distant readers will be glad to know that Farnborough Hill has not been evacuated. On the contrary, it is more full than ever. Every square inch of space is utilised, for when we reopened this September we transferred the classrooms hither from the college. The need to complete the Jubilee Hall rapidly was evident even before the official order to evacuate Hillside was given later in the summer. The proceeds of the Jubilee Fete held in May, some £337 in all, were originally intended for the purchase of an organ for the chapel, but the exigencies of the present time have obliged us to use them for the Jubilee Hall, which will now be more vitally useful

to the school than any other object.' The stoic under-statement of this account is characteristic of the spirit in which the Sisters faced both the loss of their main school buildings and the wider uncertainties of the war itself.

Farnborough Hill at war

The Second World War started in September 1939 and the effect on the school was immediate. Nearby Aldershot was the headquarters of the British army and a major airfield at Farnborough was even closer to the grounds of Hillside College. Partly to move the school away from the immediate vicinity of these potential targets, and partly because they needed the large, well-equipped buildings for the war effort, the military once again requisitioned the buildings. As *The Hillside Magazine* bears witness, a spirit of stoicism prevailed, but as Sister Wright puts it, 'It was very hard for the nuns. They had to leave a school that was well equipped – a very good gymnasium, a good-sized concert hall, an art room, pottery room, plenty of class-rooms and music cells and a lovely chapel.' As recently as the year before, improvements and new facilities had been provided, and now had to be abandoned to the army.

They did their best to improvise, but it would be another twenty-five years before they would again have a gymnasium.

The students were given an extra couple of weeks' summer holiday to make it possible to complete the move. As Mother Mostyn records in *The Story of a House*, 'Sunday 17 September 1939 was the only day Mr Brand's furniture vans were available, so we spent the day transporting all the school furniture and equipment from the college to Farnborough Hill.'

The second floor dormitory furniture was brought down and classroom furniture went up to replace it. The cellars were cleared and transformed into shelters; beds were placed in them and in the piano rooms in case of air raid alarms. St Anne's 'isolation block' was transformed into a preparatory department for younger children. For a day or two, confusion reigned. As Sister Wright, who was one of the day girls who made the move up to the Hill, remembers, 'I was fourteen. A set of huts was put up on the lawn next to the chapel for use as a gym and classrooms, and, as the number of boarders had dropped, some of the dormitories were used as classrooms. We settled in quite quickly and soon were quite at home and stopped getting lost.' For the

Extracts from Mother Horan's diary from the start of the Second World War

remaining boarders, one compensation was not having to make the long walk to the college and back six days a week.

Sporting fixtures continued, but wartime rationing meant that almost as much energy needed to be expended reaching fixtures as on the playing field itself. Sister Rennie remembers travelling by train to play another school in Guildford, walking a mile or more from the station to reach their destination and then having to repeat the process after the match was over. These matches normally took place on Saturday afternoons, after morning school had finished. The 'Games Notes' for 1942–3 (which, incidentally, list Vera Rennie in the hockey first XI, lacrosse and tennis teams) record matches against a wide range of opponents including St Mary's Ascot, St Maur's Convent, Farnham Grammar School, Royal Holloway College and the Aircraft Factory. The fact that wins outnumber losses by three to one shows that sport was taken seriously then as now. Inter-form and inter-house events were also popular and of course were much easier to arrange and attend. Even when

The war had a disastrous effect on the teaching staff as a lot of the younger women joined up. Mother Bickford took up the hem of her habit and replaced a Miss Mortimer as the sports mistress and made a very good job of it.
Janet Taylor (Griffiths)

bad weather prevented normal games, the indefatigable Mother Bickford led the girls in PT in the snow, 'which turned out to be as energetic as the stiffest game of hockey' according to the magazine.

Farnborough Hill had had a farm on site since the days of the Longmans, and even before the outbreak of war the convent had maintained a flock of chickens and other poultry and kept a small herd of cows. Sister Teresa Hawkins, who had arrived in January 1939, immediately found herself pressed into service with the herd in addition to her duties as a boarding mistress. She remembers rising at 5.30 every morning for the milking before morning Mass. Now, with wartime rationing in place, all the girls were encouraged to help with the 'dig for victory' campaign by tending individual garden plots on a strip of land adjoining the kitchen garden. The kitchen garden itself provided vegetables and fruit (pears, grapes, cherries and rhubarb) which, along with the fruit from the apple trees in the orchard, kept the school largely self-sufficient.

The flock of hens was increased so there were plenty of fresh eggs, but Sister Hawkins remembers that a brief experiment with pigs 'was not a success'. Equally unfortunate was the purchase of two nanny goats which had been advertised in *Exchange & Mart*. Mother Bickford

I started at Farnborough in 1943 when I was fifteen. I remember my parents saying goodbye to me at Waterloo station, and feeling very lonely. Fortunately (for me) a girl came and spoke to me and looked after me, and we've been friends ever since. After our evening meal (unless we had a good excuse) we all went down in the dark with torches to the 'Hut' which was a short walk away (for) about half an hour. Whenever I hear a honkey tonk piano on the radio, it brings back memories of those evenings.

As the school was so near Aldershot, the military who were based there used to come to Hillside to practise their manoeuvres, which was quite exciting for us. If there was an air raid we had to go down to the music rooms, which were a floor below (in the cellars). Wherever we went, we always had our gas masks with us. Even after all those years, when I smell rubber, I think of them.

At this time, food rationing was quite strict. We were well fed, but could always manage a bit more. There was never enough for seconds for everyone, so I think that's why I'm a quick eater now! One of the puddings we seemed to have frequently was steamed pudding (no sugar) with very watered down custard. One of my favourites (probably Sunday evenings) was fried bread topped with tinned peas! It must have been quite a job planning the menus but we all kept very well as far as I can remember.

Mother Horan was headmistress, Mother Robarts taught us French, Mother Bickford took us for hockey. I was never much good at maths, which was taught by Miss Kendall. I eventually persuaded my father to let me do cooking and sewing, which have been much more useful.

At the time I was at Farnborough petrol was very scarce, which meant my parents couldn't drive to visit me. Fortunately for them, but embarrassing for me, a food company (Brazils)

based in Amersham, where my parents lived, made weekly deliveries to the Aldershot area, so they had a lift in the van, making sure to be dropped off out of sight of the school. When I left my parents presented the school with a barometer, which was hung in the entrance hall (and is still there).

Betty Dallimore (Brunning)

hoped that they would keep the playing fields grazed without the need to resort to the petrol-mower, and supplement the milk provided by the dairy herd. Sally and Sue duly arrived and were set to work. However, it was quickly discovered that they needed new names: they were billy goats who showed little interest in grazing the playing fields and of course were incapable of providing milk. To make matters worse, they showed a Houdini-like ability to escape from their paddock and were, according to Mother Mostyn, 'exceedingly capricious in their food: in fact they ate everything except grass, even devouring portions of the nuns' habits!' So Sally and Sue were sold and instead the girls helped mow lawns by hand in the long summer evenings while Mother Shannon experimented with using the herd to keep the rough grass under control, though they too showed a tendency to stray and eventually had to be confined to their field.

The system of rationing introduced by the Ministry of Food meant that no one in wartime Britain starved, but of course many foodstuffs which had formerly been plentiful became scarce: meat, butter, eggs, flour and sugar were all rationed but, thanks to the efforts of the Sisters and helped by the ingenuity of Mother Colgan in the kitchen, the school remained well fed. Mother Mostyn writes, 'A most satisfying vegetable pie occasionally substituted for meat,

and home-made jams and carrot and ginger marmalade helped to brighten teatime and breakfast.'

Hillside College had been evacuated, not only because the military needed the facilities it provided but also because its position near the airfield was thought to make it vulnerable to attack. Farnborough Hill, with its tall tower rising above the surrounding countryside, was also a potential target, and from the air apparently provided a beacon to guide bombers to the airfield, Sandhurst and Aldershot, to name but a few obvious targets, as all the glass shone on moonlit nights. Reverend Mother Roantree was inundated with letters from parents of pupils and relatives of the nuns, begging her to evacuate everyone to the comparative safety of Ireland. After prayer and consideration, they took the advice of Bishop Cotter who told them, 'You have great devotion to the Sacred Heart and, in His name I tell you, "Stay where you are".' Despite some inevitable alarms, their confidence proved justified and the school survived the war unscathed.

Did you REALLY sleep in the music cells, and eat marmalade from carrots and sing Mass in the pitch dark...?' Oh, yes we did indeed – and much more besides. In the summer of 1940, with the threat of invasion, we repaired nightly to the music cells with precious possessions – which could mean anything from hair curlers to teddy bears, depending on age and interests – and camped on mattresses and makeshift beds, longing for an air raid so that we would perhaps be excused our homework the next day. Later, some of us slept in greater comfort under the stage of the new hall, but then the Battle of Britain ended and so life became less fraught.

Our gallant French Mademoiselle Thinon de la Troche, who used to walk the length of the refectory in formidable splendour in full evening dress each evening in order to preside over French Table, decided to return to France in June 1940 and we sang the Marseillaise with her outside the chapel before speeding her on her way. Mercifully she survived, although no news was heard of her for five long years.

Mother Colgan fiercely controlled ration books and points and carried on a personal vendetta against Hitler, somehow managing to feed us well and interestingly: carrot marmalade, rose hip jam, Woolton pie. Sister Maura splashed the hens with holy water to encourage them to lay even more eggs than was possible, while Mother Shannon prayed over each Kerry cow. Sister Farrell made potent wine in the infirmary from berries, nettles and parsley, never realising the strength of her brews so that those of us who stayed during the holidays and were treated to her concoctions were under the table before the meal had ended.

Mass in the black-out: learning all the music by heart and fumbling our way into the chapel and up to the tribune to sing. All-night vigils of prayer during times of crisis, with the priest faintly discernible by the glow of a weak torch bulb. Fire watching, two by two from the Sixth Form at night with one of the nuns, hoping for action so that we could use our skills with stirrup pumps and become heroines (and view the nuns in tin hats and gas masks!). Air raid practices, when the wardens used our grounds and we were 'wounded' and lay about with pseudo-broken limbs, waiting to be found and taken by ambulance to the casualty clearing station.

D-day. Tanks rolling along the road all night and noisy aircraft overhead. We learnt the value of prayer, with so many girls losing fathers and brothers. Already there were those whose parents had disappeared at the fall of Singapore and many old girls whose husbands had been killed.

Farnborough Hill in the war. How different it was from today, but how much of it remained calm and peaceful, thanks to the unruffled serenity and wonderful faith and devotion of Reverend Mother Roantree, Mother Horan and the community. They never transmitted their anxiety or fear, but managed to give us all a sense of security and order while chaos reigned throughout the world.

Patricia Drummond (Keane), writing in the 1977–9 magazine

Farnborough Hill girls go to war

The wartime generation of girls, who had knitted sea-boot socks and raised money for the Red Cross Fund, the Spitfire Fund and other charitable works while they were still at school, found themselves caught up in the wider war effort once they left. Mary Rose Murphy became 'an early, human computer' as she put it, helping to manipulate statistics for the RAF at the airfield in Farnborough. One of the most distinguished of these old girls was Paddy Sproule, a contemporary of Sisters Wright and Rennie and also of Miss Murphy.

Like many at the time, Paddy's exploits only became known long after they occurred. She had joined the First Aid Nursing Yeomanry in 1942, aged eighteen; her first ambition had been to drive ambulances, but at 5ft 2in tall she could not reach the pedals. Instead, after three weeks' training, she was told to go to Aylesbury, Buckinghamshire, where she would be met at the station. Her destination proved to be Grendon Hall, home of Station 53a of the SOE (Special Operations Executive). Paddy was put to work decoding signals to and from Norwegian commandos who were engaged in espionage against the Germans.

Paddy Sproule, *back*, and Mary Rose Murphy in a 1938 Lower V class photo

In July 1943 she was promoted to sergeant and sent to Algiers, to work at Inter-Services Signal Unit 6 from where agents and arms were sent into southern France and Italy to carry out guerrilla activity and to wear down German forces in preparation for the Allied landings. While there, she was one of four SOE officers encoding and deciphering all the messages between London, the Italian forces and a British agent in the weeks leading up to the Italian armistice. This involved moving rapidly between three separate codes, one each for the three parties concerned.

Further promotions followed and she was sent first to Italy with the SOE and later to London, where she worked for the famous codebreaker Leo Marks, helping to break many messages classed as 'indecipherables'. In the final days of the war in Europe, she was posted to Calcutta where she was put in charge of the SOE cipher office. Her last act in the office was burning the codes and files after VJ Day. Her achievements were such that they merited a high profile obituary in the *Daily Telegraph* on her death in 2010.

The Polish icon of Czestochowa in the school library

As a precaution, however, mattresses were spread on the floor of the music practice rooms in the cellars, and during air raids, girls would retreat there until the all-clear sounded. If the alarm came at night, Sister Hawkins, in charge of the younger girls' dormitory, instructed the girls to grab onto one another's nightgowns in a line with the lead girl holding onto hers so that they could make their way quickly and safely through the darkened building – 'like elephants', as she described it later. Girls had to bring pillows and eiderdowns with them and try to sleep where they could, but Sister Hawkins remembers that they never complained nor used the interrupted nights as an excuse not to work. They all became expert at listening for the sounds of German engines and distinguishing them from those of the British planes. The arrival of the school caretaker, William Johns, with the tea urn in the morning was a welcome sight to all. And, as blacking out so many windows, especially in buildings as large as the school

chapel, proved impossible, as Mother Mostyn put it, 'we prayed in the dark throughout the war.'

Ann Yarnold, later a member of staff, remembered the clothes rationing which made uniforms precious and difficult to replace: 'School uniform was difficult to obtain and had to last. The rather attractive brown and white check dresses worn by the "browns" in summer became unobtainable. I had one of the few remaining ones and, of course, managed to catch it on a fence and tear a large hole. There was no similar material to mend it, but Mother Horan come to the rescue with the original pattern piece enclosed in cardboard – just enough to cover the gap. In spite of wartime conditions, dress was still formal. We had to wear hats on all journeys and gloves were obligatory. A prefect or member of staff was liable to emerge from the bushes on the front drive and ask home-going day girls why they were not wearing them. The staff wore their graduate gowns, which I confused with the nuns' habits and told my parents that my class teacher was gradually becoming a nun.'

With the fall of Poland, Britain saw an influx of Polish refugees and Farnborough Hill took some of them in, including the daughters of Count Balinski-Jundzill, who was secretary to the Polish Educational Research Council. Mother Mostyn recounts how the parents of these girls later clubbed together to present the school with a very

> I was there through the war years ... the rhododendrons and azaleas on the driveway up to the Hill were only small bushes and there were no fences or walkways and traffic was not one way! You could see the Chapel across the grounds from the front gate.
> *Helen Campbell (Fermie)*

Barbara Howells (Zamoyska) and friends in lacrosse kit and blazers

fine copy of Our Lady, Queen of Poland, the icon of Czestochowa, which still hangs in the school library. For years the Polish girls had a tea party under it on their national feast day.

Ann Yarnold remembered the arrival of the Polish refugees, 'with stories of escapes from the ruins of Warsaw or from prison camps. I remember that they all seemed talented either academically or artistically. The most famous Polish exile, however, arrived after the war. I was one of Mme Mikolajewska's first Sixth Form Latin pupils, in the early days of her (struggles with) English. "Say me please why you laugh" she would order as she conducted us through Aeneas's adventures in "the underground" where the Furies appeared in "bloody shorts", but in spite of our amusement we greatly respected the scholarship that had led to her achievements.' Although her English remained eccentric, Mme Knickerelastic, as she was known to generations of girls, continued to terrify and inspire in equal measure until her retirement in 1979.

Radio was a vital source of information about the war, and one particular broadcast remains in Sister Rennie's memory. The Red Cross read out lists of those captured, and one girl at the school learned that her father had been taken prisoner by the Japanese in this way; it was a terrible shock. A 'Condolences' column became a regular feature of *The Hillside Magazine*. The 1943–4 edition, for example, recorded the death of Miss Morton's brother, killed in action, and two girls' brothers, Tony Vaughan, killed in India, and John Fear Hill, killed in Italy.

I was taken on at reduced boarding school fees, 'as a mark of sympathy for the Polish nation.' Many aspects that I enjoyed included gymnastics, dancing and swimming, together with games such as lacrosse, netball, hockey and tennis. There were many of us Polish girls in my year and we used to occasionally perform Polish dances on the lawn.

Barbara Howells (Zamoyska)

Girls in traditional Polish dress

Telephone 97 Farnborough, Hants.

Hillside Convent College
Farnborough Hill
Hampshire

7th May, 1946.

Dear Madame Zamoyska,

I have asked the Trustees to accept your offer of £25 per term as fees for Barbara, and they have asked me to tell you that they will accept them as a mark of sympathy for the Polish Nation. I shall therefore be happy to welcome Barbara as a pupil in September, and hope that she will be very happy here.

I am enclosing a uniform list, as it is well to begin thinking about these things in good time these days. With all kind remembrances and good wishes,

Yours sincerely in J.C.,

(Mother Superior)

Sisters in the school kitchens with the old cooking range and coal-fired ovens behind them, 1940s

Peace at last

Nearly six years of conflict in Europe finally came to an end in May 1945. Jane Thorne, a fourth former at the time, records in the school magazine how 'wirelesses were never switched off – everyone was tensely waiting for the official announcement to come from London'. Molly Foster, Patricia Fowler and Susan Ellis give a graphic account of the mounting excitement at school:

'During evening recreation on Monday 7 May, a rumour went round that Reverend Mother had heard on the wireless that peace had been declared. Was it really true? Excitement was intense. At nine o'clock we trooped down to the hall to listen to the news. Peals of laughter echoed through the rooms and corridors as we passed, and in the hall itself girls were dancing up and down, tearing to and fro or lying exhausted on the ground. Suddenly we were silent. The bells of Big Ben pealed out – one, two, three and slowly on to nine. Then "This is London calling…" Breathlessly we listened; the atmosphere was tense as we awaited the longed-for news. It came at last – peace!

'The next day we all got up for an eight o'clock Mass – a Mass of Thanksgiving of course! Then what a great surprise awaited us as we went into the refectory for breakfast – flags were flying, coloured balls and ribbons decorated the room and all the tables were arranged in Vs. Then came bacon and eggs for everyone. We wondered how ever Sister had been able to get such a breakfast ready without staying up all night! We did hear afterwards that some of the nuns had stayed up very late with the prefects doing the decorations.

'All school rules were lifted and during the first part of the morning we rushed around the house and grounds at liberty to go any and everywhere. The tennis courts were crowded and rounders was in full swing. Just before lunch we all went upstairs and changed into our cool, fresh summer dresses. What a beautiful sight at lunch – red, yellow, blue, green, in fact every conceivable colour made the room brighter and homelier than ever. The menu, which was printed on each table, was most amusing, especially "Berlin cabbage". Other items were Potage de Pois Victoire, Rosbif d'Angleterre, Tomates de Russe, Sauce a l'Amerique, Trifle Churchillian and Vin Truman! The last item was made by Sister Farrell and didn't we enjoy it!

'After a short rest we went out again, the seniors to play tennis, the juniors to have rides in Polly's (the school pony) cart. Then at three o'clock we listened to the Right Honourable Winston Churchill. Tea at four was followed by Benediction at which we sang the "Te Deum" in Thanksgiving.'

The celebrations continued with a film in the rectory, supper (hard boiled eggs decorated with Vs), dancing and then finally a bonfire down on the hockey practice pitch. Next day was tennis and horse riding in the grounds followed by an impromptu bazaar in the hall, with the proceeds going towards 'Masses which were offered during the next two weeks for all parents and relatives (of the girls past and present) who had lost their lives during the war'.

The breathless account concluded by reflecting that 'it is only a beginning of peace and there is much still to be done, we know, but before we do anything in the line of having a good holiday we should stop and thank God for all He has done for us, for without His help we know we should have been defeated and ruined, so Deo Gratias!'

Post-war expansion

While the number of boarders had dropped at the start of the war, by the time it ended the expansion of the school had become so marked that the nuns were forced to contemplate separating the juniors from the senior and middle school. During the war the juniors had been housed in Rosary Lodge, near the foot of the hill, but now Mother Roantree began the search for a much larger building. In 1946, the Order bought Yateley Hall, about six miles from Farnborough, a beautiful old house of rose-coloured brick which had once been a pre-Reformation nunnery and hostel for pilgrims. It became the Yateley Hall Preparatory Boarding School for Farnborough Hill, and served as a feeder school for Farnborough Hill itself until its closure in the 1980s.

By 1951 the day preparatory school had outgrown Rosary Lodge, even with the addition of one of the now infamous army huts. Mother Roantree proceeded to buy White Friars, a beautiful stone-built bungalow-type house with large grounds in Avenue Road. After it had been blessed by Bishop King, who celebrated its first Mass in the new assembly hall, the 'preps' moved in and the school continued to grow. Michael Lehman, who has had a long-standing familial and geographical connection with Farnborough Hill, remembers his time there very fondly under the watchful eye of the headmistress, Mother Fox. He remembers her clearly as being very strict but understanding of young people; she wanted pupils to be able to achieve highly for themselves. He was also taught deportment by Farnborough Hill old girl Mary Rose Murphy, and described how she always stood straight with her hands behind her back whatever was going on around her, completely unfazed by the hectic behaviour of the boisterous preps. White Friars eventually became St Patrick's Primary School and the remaining White Friars pupils were transferred to Yateley Hall.

In Yateley itself, the post-war building boom increased the demand for day school places for local children, while

as the 1950s and 1960s progressed fewer young children were sent to board. As a result, boarding was phased out at Yateley Hall with the remaining girls sent to live at Farnborough Hill. As Sister Eileen Grant recounts: 'In 1962/3, extensive repairs and alterations were made to all the rooms above the kitchen and the school cloakroom area. At first these were used as classrooms and a library, but when in the late 1960s the boarders were phased out, these rooms were converted into bedrooms and a sitting-room for the Sisters. For their last year, the final few boarders were housed at Farnborough Hill and travelled each day to Yateley Hall for lessons.'

Above left: Yateley Hall

Above: Mixed juniors, probably at White Friars

Left: The opening of White Friars, 1948

Below: Corpus Christi procession at Yateley Hall, 1956

Melissa Troup's bronze statue of the Madonna and Child in the lower gallery

in January 1946, they opened their regular Sunday Mass to the Catholics of the area and they remained involved in a wide range of religious and social activities. The Pelly Concert Orchestra is named after Mother Pelly, who played second violin.

In 1982, dwindling numbers meant that the Sisters had to leave Yateley Hall, though the parents continued to run the school until 1985, when it finally closed. The building has now been converted into a block of flats, but a beautiful bronze statue of a Madonna and Child, created by a pupil at Farnborough Hill, continues to stand in the grounds. Another copy of the statue stands in the lower gallery of Farnborough Hill as a reminder of this past association.

The blessings of peace

After the end of the First World War the Order had been able to return to their requisitioned premises at Hillside College. This time, however, they decided to remain at Farnborough Hill. According to Sister Rennie, it was a matter of convenience. Farnborough Road was no longer the country lane it had been in the 1930s, and the prospect of marching boarders down the road to lessons while coping with the increased traffic and noise on the main road became steadily less attractive. Then, too, there was the convenience of having everyone on the same site and able to have all their lessons together, instead of having to duplicate afternoon games and handicraft lessons. By the time the Ministry of Defence was ready to relinquish Hillside, nearly ten years had passed since the enforced move up the hill and they were used to being there together.

Just after the end of the war there were approximately 160 boarders and 90 day girls, divided into two forms per year according to how well they had done in the Common Entrance examination. The brighter students were in the A classes, while the less able were in the 'plain' classes, eg I and IA. There was some movement between the two streams, but on the whole students' position in the school was determined from the outset, with very different expectations of the different groups. This, of course, was also the era of the grammar school and secondary moderns, so such streaming would have seemed perfectly normal to most parents and pupils.

Yateley Hall continued as a day school, and the numbers went up. Various changes took place over the next few years. At one stage, for a few years, the education authority allowed the school to accept pupils up to the age of thirteen. Children as young as four were accepted in a pre-kindergarten class, and boys up to age seven or eight were also accepted. Later the boys could stay on until the eleven-plus. There was even a boys' football team, coached by a 'striker' from Aldershot Town Football Club. Farnborough Hill, or at least its sister school, can therefore legitimately claim to have old boys as well as old girls.

Yateley Hall and its small community of nuns played an important part in local religious life. From their first arrival

An advertisement for Hillside Convent, pre-1927

Hillside Convent

(THE SYCAMORES)

FARNBOROUGH PARK

'Phone: 97 Farnborough

1. High-Class Boarding School for Girls (THE SYCAMORES).

2. College and High School for Girls (FARNBOROUGH ROAD).

3. Preparatory School for Girls and Boys (FARNBOROUGH ROAD).

The Course of Studies comprises all the branches of a superior English Education. The Pupils are prepared for the University Examinations, Oxford Locals, the Associated Board of the Royal Academy and Royal College of Music, and Art Certificates.*

Aldershot and Camberley 'Buses pass the Schools. A Special School 'Bus leaves Aldershot at 8.30 a.m. and leaves the High School at 1.30 p.m.

FOR PARTICULARS APPLY TO THE REVEREND MOTHER SUPERIOR.

* Special facilities for acquiring Modern Languages. Private lessons given.

Left: The hexagonal rooms of the new classroom block today

Inset: The block during construction, 1953

To accommodate the increasing numbers, a new classroom block was planned, parallel with the chapel and attached at one end to the Jubilee wing, forming a three-sided courtyard. The original plan had been to connect it to the chapel by means of a covered walkway; an extension alongside the chapel had also been planned for, by leaving bricks at either end jutting out, to facilitate 'keying-in'. Only in 2013 was this part of the plan put into action, with the construction of a new music suite alongside the chapel. Twenty-first-century students, meanwhile, have grown used to the apparently random existence of a door in Room 12 to the lawn outside. This is all that exists of the planned walkway; according to the original plans, Room 12 was to be a cloakroom and the door would originally have been a wide arch, as can be seen from outside.

The urgent need to provide housing and repair buildings damaged in the war meant that the new classroom block did not get underway until 1952. Once more Adrian Gilbert Scott drew up the plans and supervised the building work. Mother Roantree was not well enough to play an active role, but she supported Mother Horan in pursing this project. The two end rooms, hexagonal in shape, were intended for common rooms and were supplied with oak cupboards and window seat lockers, with oak panelling above. Nevertheless they were used as classrooms as well, and the new block was occupied in September 1953. In addition, as Patricia Sketchley wrote, 'The Sixth and Fifth Forms were delighted to find themselves the proud possessors of two lovely common rooms. The Hut was quite unrecognisable,

The blind arch surrounding the door to Room 12

having been transformed into a junior common room and a needlework room.'

1952 saw the end of an era with the death of Reverend Mother Roantree (see box). Several generations of the Roantree family attended Farnborough Hill, beginning with the daughters of two of Mother Roantree's brothers: Norah, Mary (a head girl), Irene (who designed the school uniform in the 1930s), Gwendoline, Helen, Eliza and Patricia. Norah's daughter, Jane Broxham (Martin-Murphy), arrived at Farnborough Hill in 1949 after two years at Yateley Hall. Mother Roantree was bedridden and quite elderly when Jane arrived, and she found herself pressed into service as a reader every afternoon. These sessions, when she would sit in a chair next to her great-aunt's bed, provided a welcome alternative to the games field, and Jane worked her way through many classic works of literature.

Jane's experience was typical of boarders from overseas at the time in that she was expected to stay at school over the Easter holidays, so that from the time she arrived in January after the Christmas break to the end of term in the summer, she never left the grounds of the school except to attend occasional medical appointments. They lived in an enclosed world, while the day girls went to and from their family homes and had much more freedom at weekends. This may partly account for the undoubted tensions which sometimes arose between the two groups. Saturday

The Roantree family. Norah, *right*, and her sister Irene, *centre right*, who designed the school blazer and badge in the 1930s, with their cousins Eliza, *centre left*, and Patricia, *left*

Reverend Mother Roantree

In August 1952 Mother Roantree, Mother Superior, one of the founders of the original school at Hillside and the person, above all others, who had shaped and nurtured the growing school, died. She was ninety and had been a nun for sixty-eight years. Sister Wright remembers her well, both from her days as a pupil at the school and later as a young nun. The phrase she felt best summed her up was 'very regal'. In the Hillside days, Mother Roantree would be driven over once a week to present medals to the children who had come top in the class that week. The pupils would sit cross-legged on the floor of the hall until it was their turn, and then curtsey to her before being presented with their medals. Sister Wright remembers that everyone had great respect for her; she was 'not frightening' but 'at the top of the ladder' and 'very well in with everybody – a great organiser who always went for the best and expected high standards from everyone'. This is reflected in the vision which led her to engage the services of one of the leading architects of the day to design a school chapel and build it on such a grand scale. Even in her later years, when her sight was failing, she was still observant of those around her and would quietly point out anything she felt needed to be put right. She, and the other Sisters like her, are remembered by Sister Wright as 'all very kind. They never stood any nonsense, but everyone loved them.'

Mother Roantree's funeral was held in the chapel which she had dreamed of when she first came to Farnborough Hill. It was attended by many members of the clergy and celebrated by the Bishop of Portsmouth. She is buried in the community cemetery in the grounds, surrounded by the graves of the Sisters whom she had led and inspired for so many years. As a memorial to her, a modern set of Stations of the Cross was installed in the chapel. These were carved by Michael Clarke and paid for by a subscription in her memory. A memorial scholarship was also offered, and in the autumn of 1953 a marble cross and tombstone were placed on her grave with the inscription 'Mulier Fortis' ('strong woman').

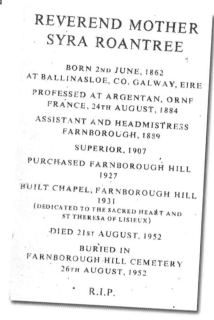

REVEREND MOTHER
SYRA ROANTREE

BORN 2ND JUNE, 1862
AT BALLINASLOE, CO. GALWAY, EIRE

PROFESSED AT ARGENTAN, ORNE
FRANCE, 24TH AUGUST, 1884

ASSISTANT AND HEADMISTRESS
FARNBOROUGH, 1889

SUPERIOR, 1907

PURCHASED FARNBOROUGH HILL
1927

BUILT CHAPEL, FARNBOROUGH HILL
1931
(DEDICATED TO THE SACRED HEART AND
ST THERESA OF LISIEUX)

DIED 21ST AUGUST, 1952

BURIED IN
FARNBOROUGH-HILL CEMETERY
26TH AUGUST, 1952

R.I.P.

Funeral announcement, 1952

shopping trips were yet to feature in the weekly routine of boarding life, though of course the sports teams made trips out to play against other schools.

Daily life was tightly regulated. The boarders were woken early for Mass, then had breakfast in the refectory, seated at long tables presided over by a teacher and not allowed to speak unless spoken to. They then went back upstairs to make beds and tidy the dormitory, ready for the daily inspection. Assembly followed in the school hall, and then it was off to lessons, played out with stirring music. At break they had a small bottle of milk and a bun and could amuse themselves in the quad or go outside if the weather permitted. Lunch was again eaten in the refectory under the stern eye of a teacher. The rule about clearing their plates was so rigidly enforced that, it was claimed, 'we had to eat the greenfly on the lettuce'. Jane Broxham (Martin-Murphy) remembers one practical joke. Someone passed a jar of jam to the teacher at their table, pretending that it was sauce for the fish. The victim, having unwittingly spread her fish with jam, proceeded to eat it without comment or retribution. On Sunday evenings in summer, as a treat, they would be given a meal consisting of a cold fried egg sandwiched between two pieces of toast and were allowed to eat it outside informally on the cloister lawn.

When afternoon school ended, they were allowed up to the dormitories to change into their own choice of clothes before the evening activities, though they were expected to sponge down their skirts and hang them over the bedside chairs to air before they returned downstairs for prep and tea. Baths were now limited to two nights a week by rota, and the hot water system made a terrible noise as the bath filled. The hot water could run out, too, so there was an incentive to be first in the queue. Jane Broxham's mother sent her to school with a stock of long, old-fashioned night gowns and she was mortified to find that all the other girls in her dormitory wore pyjamas. She got round this problem by changing in the bathroom after all the others had got into bed and creeping in after the lights were out.

Farnborough Hill animals

Sally and Sue, the misnamed billy goats who arrived at Farnborough Hill at the beginning of the war, were not the school's only memorable animals. In recent years, girls were familiar with the sight of Missie the border collie accompanying her master, David Bell (who sadly died in 2014), as he worked in the school grounds. Earlier generations of girls knew Trixie, owned by Sister Cahill. Sister Wright remembers that one of her frequent tasks, as a young novice, was taking Trixie for a run around the grounds, allowing both of them to let off steam. Toby, another school dog, was charmingly described by Martina Bayley of Form IA in the magazine of 1955–6: 'Toby is the school dog; he is a little fat but very handsome, although in need of that extra brushing. Toby is really very good-tempered, but he does like peace and quiet while he is making his repast on some juicy bone. He is very tolerant when noisy girls dash up and down the bank on which he is dozing, but he would prefer it if they didn't. He likes to lie on the carpet in the middle of the chapel corridor, and when the girls file into chapel he examines their shoes... He is getting on in years now, though we hope that he will live to see many more generations of Farnborough girls, for we all love him.' Toby's main role in the life of the school was to help round up the herd of Kerry cows morning and evening for milking.

Sister Cahill with Trixie

Rory, the black and white school cat, was another memorable character. One Christmas he was found fast asleep in the Nativity crib, on top of Baby Jesus. He sensed that Mother Horan did not altogether approve of him and was in the habit of leaving freshly caught mice on the floor outside her bedroom in the mornings. He also kept the Sisters company when they said the rosary in the grounds in the summer.

Rory was obviously a favourite with the boarders. Nicole Turle of Form IV described him 'taking his leisure on one of the refectory radiators, dusting it thoughtfully with his tail from time to time... At mealtimes Rory is rarely absent. At breakfast and tea, especially when there is milk to be had... he has been known to jump unobtrusively onto the chair and be presented with a saucer of milk... His good deed for the day consists of an occasional visit to the sick in the infirmary... (He) is most particular about where he sleeps. He deems the... red corridor highly satisfactory, and would like always to sleep curled up in bed with one of his many doting admirers.'

Judy Horne, writing in 1955, reports that 'Christopher Robin... has now had to be rechristened Christina Robina owing to a happy event. She had three lovely kittens, making a total of seven cats including Rory.'

The same report notes the continued presence of cows on the estate but opens with an account of the premature death of Frisca, the Irish donkey. Frisca, whose name reflected her arrival on the Feast of St Francis, was purchased to help on the farm alongside Polly the pony. With petrol still scarce and expensive, the nuns used pony and donkey power to pull the laundry baskets up and down the hill and transport the heavy baskets of apples from the orchard in the autumn. Sadly, Frisca fell victim to the girls' misguided kindness and developed laminitis after eating too many buns. She made her own particular contribution to the funeral of Mother Roantree in 1952. As the funeral procession was making its way down the front drive from the chapel to the nuns' graveyard, she came over to the fence which bordered the drive and gave the loudest and longest bray anyone had heard. It lightened the mood of what was a very sad and solemn occasion.

I was at Farnborough Hill as a boarder 1958–64, and thought I'd landed in heaven! My family had recently converted to Catholicism and the daily ritual of going to early Mass in that beautiful, soaring chapel, all wearing white veils which we then hung over the backs of our chairs afterwards at breakfast, is a memory firmly imprinted in my mind. I later joined the chapel choir and learnt many motets and Masses which have stayed with me. An important novelty which we had to accomplish as new girls was the curtsey-on-the-move. You had to curtsey if you passed Reverend Mother with a visitor; the foot nearest to whoever was owed the curtsey had to go behind the other and you'd bob down while still walking. It was imperative to get the correct foot behind, otherwise you'd trip up.

I enjoyed so many things, particularly the sport and drama. It was wonderful just to step out of the quad where we had games lockers, and straight down the hill to the games field, or, in the summer, to the tennis courts. I remember revising for exams lying on the games field one hot summer, too, while the highlight of that term was the school play or operetta. The Fifth and Sixth

Forms did not go home after exams as they do now in most schools, but were there for the full summer term.'

I was one of the naughtiest girls in the school and I'm not sure why, other than I had read too many silly stories about midnight feasts. We had several of those, during one of which we climbed down a fire escape outside a dormitory window, a potentially dangerous undertaking.
Julia Ashenden (Ross Williamson)

Diana Eady

Diana Eady, one of those whose parents lived abroad, was a lively girl who could be counted upon to interrupt dull lessons by pushing her pencil box to the floor so that they could all scramble around picking them up. Jane Broxham (Martin-Murphy) vividly remembers travelling up to Waterloo with her at the start of the Easter holidays, Jane bound for Ireland and Diana for Egypt via Italy. Jane remembers how the two girls discussed their journeys and how she envied Diana for travelling on one of the new Comet aircraft, while she was due to fly on a much less up-to-date plane. When she reached home, Jane was horrified to hear of the loss of the plane Diana had been travelling on. It had suffered metal fatigue and broken apart off Naples. Diana was one of only two passengers whose bodies were found. Diana Frisby described Diana as 'great fun and a born actress'. Of the crash she says, 'I don't think any of us had experienced a loss like that and we were quite traumatised … we still talk about her.'

The shock of this event is evident in the obituary of Diana in the school magazine: 'When we heard that the plane was missing (on 8 April 1954), a cloud of sadness settled upon the house as we thought of her parents and the terrible anxiety that they must be enduring. We learned that her body had been rescued, that death had been immediate and most of all we knew that Diana had been to Mass and Holy Communion here on the Wednesday morning before beginning her journey… We shall remember Diana as we always saw her, and as we saw her for the last time, brown eyes sparkling, her face alight with happiness, a smile on her lips and a pleasant word for all of us as she said good-bye. She came to us a refreshingly happy child, she led a happy life and she has surely entered into a happy eternity.' Many Masses were said in Diana's memory and her heartbroken parents donated a beautiful oak prie-dieu for the Lady Chapel, where it still remains. Ironically, the air accident investigation which determined the cause of the crash – metal fatigue – was carried out at the RAE in Farnborough.

Mother Horan, the headmistress, built on the growing success of the school by promoting sciences as well as arts subjects, and successfully negotiated with Hampshire County Education Office for the seniors to attend practical chemistry classes at Farnborough Grammar School. She enlarged the Sixth Form and increased the number of university entrants, even at a time when opportunities for female students were only a fraction of those open to their male counterparts. Mother Horan also received an invitation from the Archbishop of Dublin to establish a convent school in the growing suburb of Terenure, which opened in 1953. This was later joined by a boarding school in Clermont in Co Wicklow, and the Sisters of the community moved between these linked educational

My dear Mummy and Daddy, from whom did you hear, from more than one source, about my behaviour, Daddy? It wasn't all my fault anyway; I only said I'd take the blame for the stink-bomb, I didn't let it off. The sneezing powder also, that wasn't all my fault; of course that Mother Burke, she blames me for everything. If I'm in her dormitory next term (if I'm still here), I shall not go in there. My behaviour was not foolish and rude: I wasn't rude to anybody.

I am no longer form captain because of those incidents. If these nuns didn't nag at me so much I might be able to get somewhere. Daddy, I have been trying terribly hard since my rudeness last year, but these nuns make me rude. I do not want you to waste your money on me here, if you don't think I'm working, but I'm jolly well doing my best. I think it's perfectly unfair not letting me go to stay with Tessa. Please, if I do improve, will you please let me go to stay with her?

What do you mean by my 'childish pranks' with mistresses and prefects? As far as I know I have not played any pranks on any prefects. I went to Mother Hogan immediately I received your letter Daddy, and told her I was sorry. She said I had been so much better at the beginning of term, and she asked me who caused the trouble in Mother Burke's dormitory, because she knew it wasn't always me. I told her exactly what I thought of Mother Burke. She told me to try very hard until the end of term. I told her also that you were thinking of taking me away.

I have done badly in exams again this term. I've been trying so hard to get good results, but it didn't work. My lowest mark is 21% and my highest is 47%. I did so much revision too (but) your letter put me off the exams, Daddy; I couldn't concentrate as I was upset.

Mary Clemow, a letter of June 1955

Mary's parents did not take her away, but her resolution to behave proved short-lived. By the following November, Mother Moore was writing to Brigadier Clemow to tell him that Mary was suspended until the end of term because she and 'another girl were missing shortly after 2.30 this afternoon and they remained away for four hours. It appears they went to the cinema.' Perhaps surprisingly, Mary Clemow reports that she and Mother Burke became great friends in later years; she came to appreciate how hard the nuns worked, often teaching all day and then supervising teenage girls all night.

Above: A nun taking an RE class in the 1950s in the new block (Room 13)

Right: Mother Alexander inspecting students' work in an art class held in one of the temporary huts

Ode to the Nuns of Farnborough Hill
Mary Clemow, 1955

To the tune of 'Sweet Lass of Richmond Hill'

The Farnborough Hill Community
Put up with our defection
We help them unawares along
The ladder of perfection,
We're perfect beasts
With midnight feasts
And show a good selection
Of faults that would drive everyone
Less patient to distraction.

CHORUS:
Oh Nuns of Farnborough Hill
Oh Nuns of Farnborough Hill
We'll not forget, we won't regret
Our years at Farnborough Hill.

We're late for meals
And then burst in
Like stormy force nine gales
And if you're near the hall
You can, a deafening room assails.
We mark the floors and kick the doors
And all reminding fails
To make us tidy up the quad
Or put away our veils.

CHORUS

However scatty we may be
There's one day in the year
And all our best intentions go
To keep you free from care.
We try to show that you may know
We always will remember
To carry out your wishes on
The twenty first of November.

CHORUS

establishments. The number of overseas boarders also grew, not just from Ireland but from further afield as well. Jane Broxham (Martin-Murphy) remembers quite a few from South America, sent for an English Catholic education. These girls seemed terribly glamorous to their contemporaries.

Alongside the academic developments recorded in the magazines of the postwar era are glimpses of the world beyond. Royal events are recorded, with special mention of the wedding of Princess Elizabeth in 1947, the death of the King in 1952 and the coronation of the new Queen the following year. And as the war and wartime restrictions receded, travel became possible once more and the magazine featured travel articles written by some of the pupils: 'A Danish farm', 'Annecy and its lake', 'Kronborg'. One reason for this increased mobility was the number of parents living and working overseas.

Individual nuns were very kind but, though very concerned with spiritual life, the school did not offer much in the way of pastoral care or affection. The 'facts of life' were never discussed and it was expected that older girls would look after younger ones. The atmosphere was hierarchial. As Jane Broxham put it, 'Your girls have voices; we had no voice.' Towards the end of her time at the school the library began stocking a daily paper, but on the whole the outside world was kept at arm's length. Contact with boys was strictly limited; one day girl remembers being told off for cycling home from school with her brother, in case a passer-by misinterpreted their relationship.

One exception to the 'no boys' rule was the annual dance at the Dorchester Hotel in London with cadets from Sandhurst. The Sixth Form girls selected for the outing were summoned the evening before for a lecture by Mother Horan. She reminded them that they were representing the school and should not do anything to bring discredit. They could accept one glass of sherry, but must decline if a second was offered. She finished off by telling them to 'always keep your white gloves on'. One girl notably overstepped the mark while at the dance, and when called upon to explain herself said 'but I kept my white gloves on'. Ann James (Tomaline) also remembers occasional dances with local boys, strictly supervised by the nuns. Before they could attend the girls had to have their dresses inspected 'to make sure they were not too low in the front'.

Handicrafts and needlework as well as games played a large part in the curriculum and music was much encouraged. However, the music practice rooms in the cellar were dismal and Mother Fehrenbach used to enforce concentration by poking the less enthusiastic smartly in the back with a pencil. Some girls went on to take degrees at Oxford or Cambridge or to study medicine or nursing, and there was a general expectation that they were being prepared for work as well as motherhood, but there was much less emphasis on the academic then. 'Farnborough Hill girls can't spell' was a frequent charge. Nevertheless, many girls who attended the school in that period remember their school days fondly and went on to have interesting and fulfilling lives.

Mother Horan

I was at Farnborough between 1957 and 1964. I arrived the term of my twelfth birthday and left aged just nineteen, because I stayed on for the autumn term after my A levels to do the Oxbridge entrance exams. Thus my time at the school was a formative period of my life. Inevitably, certain teachers loom large in the memory, especially Mlle Charbonneau who taught us French and Mme Mikolajewska who taught us Latin. They were formidable personalities. Mlle Charbonneau, who had lost her fiancé during the war when she was studying in England, decided to settle in this country – but she remained entirely French, both in her dress and in her mannerisms. She had a gift for teaching and kept order among us by natural authority and a certain eccentric delivery, which we loved to imitate behind her back.

Mme Mikolajewska, on the other hand, terrified us and we lived in an atmosphere of fear during Latin lessons. We respected her but did not love her. This might have been because of her Polish style of pedagogy: she had a PhD from Warsaw and had come over as a refugee during the war. She brought with her rigid standards of scholarship, heavily accented English and a fierce manner with girls who had failed to learn their Latin verbs for homework. As I did Latin A level, she followed me up the school, with her blue rinse hairstyles, her sardonic comments and her severe, pre-war Polish clothes.

Another teacher who was also a 'character' was Miss Dashper who taught us dancing; she was wiry, very energetic, with an imperious voice; she would tolerate no slacking in the hall where we had our classes. Like Mlle Charbonneau, her fiancé, who had been in the Air Force, was killed in the war. We learnt this only when a classmate had the temerity to ask her why she always wore an Air Force badge pinned to her dress. She once found me reading a book about the Holocaust and said tersely: 'Yes, you need to know about it.' At the time, in the late 1950s, we had very little sense of what suffering the war had brought with it, even though it had clearly affected the lives of several members of staff. The First World War also had its witness: an ancient school gardener who had been in the trenches, and who always used to greet us with 'Keep smiling, my dears!'

Outside lessons, I have many memories of the school chapel. In the Fourth Form I shared a bedroom with three other girls; we were woken at 6.50 sharp by Mother Hawkins, the dormitory mistress, cheerfully intoning 'Benedicamus Domino' to which we responded reluctantly 'Deo gratias' as we got ready for daily Mass at 7.30, our white veils pinned on with Kirby grips. In the Sixth Form we senior girls used to take turns for the daunting honour of making the Mass responses from a prie-dieu outside the sanctuary. On Saturday evenings we always sang the 'Salve Regina' in the darkened chapel and on Sundays, in the chapel choir, we learned to sing the most beautiful motets and Masses.

I have many other warm memories: watching old black and white films, like *Scott's Last Expedition* and *Great Expectations* on an ancient projector in the hall as a Saturday evening treat; slipping out of the school grounds near the playing fields to buy sweets at the corner shop; entertaining the residents of the Cheshire Home who came for our Corpus Christi processions; our annual school seaside trip to Climping; trying to make conversation with the teachers who sat at the head of the tables at lunchtime in the refectory; buying holy pictures and tuck from Mother Tiernan in her little shop on Saturday mornings; wangling a day in the infirmary on the pretence that I had lost my voice; eating fresh bread rolls at breakfast before classes; late-night conversations with friends in 'the flat' where we had study bedrooms in our final year. Looking back, I can see now that it was a privileged period of my life – though at the time I took it all for granted.

Frances Phillips (Cargin)

Left: The Sixth Form ready for the Beaumont dance, 1950s

Right: A letter from Dickins and Jones to a student, 1962

DICKINS AND JONES
LIMITED
REGENT STREET · LONDON W.I

Telegrams
DERANJAY, WESDO, LONDON

Telephone
REGENT · 7070

In reply
please quote
MO/229

30th March, 1962

Dear Madam,

　　　　Under separate cover we have sent you at the request of your Mother a 3 piece suit and we hope it will meet with your satisfaction and be the right fitting. If you would prefer it in brown/lemon or in a smaller size please let us know.

　　　　Yours faithfully

　　　　R.B. German
　　　　Manager, Mail Order Department

FDB/AB

Miss. G. McElligott,
Farnborough Hill Convent,
Farnborough,
Hants.

'A school that can boast a strong artistic tradition': music and drama

Music and drama have always played an important part in the life of Farnborough Hill. Generations of girls have sung Mass settings in the chapel, taken part in formal and informal concerts and practised their instruments in rooms ranging from the Empress's grand salon to the subterranean music practice rooms. Drama too has taken place in the school hall, on the lawns, in the chapel, in the school theatre and in countless classrooms and corridors. The long tradition of performing musicals has blended the two, but each exists separately with its own traditions and facilities.

A beautiful hand-written programme of the 'Distribution annuelle des prix', or annual prize giving ceremony for Hillside College in 1904 lists a piano duet, a violin solo, a solo 'chant' and an orchestral piece. The Empress Eugenie, still very much in residence up the hill, was the guest of honour and it is clear that the Sisters were anxious to show her the school's musicians at their best. The same spirit was evident in the festivities twenty years later, which marked the reopening of the college on 28 July 1924 after a decade in the hands of the army. The Bishop of Portsmouth was treated to a varied programme ranging from a 'sextett' (*sic*) for strings titled 'Fantazia', through a selection of traditional English songs and recitations and finishing with an 'Andante and Minuet' by Dittersdorf and a rousing rendition of 'God Save the King'. The bishop also celebrated Benediction in the school chapel.

Opposite:
An exploration of Jacobean theatre by A level students in 2002

Right: Drama in the woods at Hillside, 1930s

The twin traditions of secular and sacred music at the school were clearly well established by then. The following day the day students also held a concert for their parents. As with sport, music lessons took place in the afternoon so the 'blues' and the 'browns' often performed separately, especially as many concerts were house events and houses were separate as well. The 'blues' performed a Nativity play for the Christmas prize giving ceremony that year, for example.

Boarders and day girls marched into and out of morning Assembly at Hillside to rousing music, sometimes recorded Souza marches and sometimes live pieces played by talented soloists. Although recorded music was available, playing a musical instrument was much prized as a social skill; family concert parties were still relatively common at that time. The prize giving concerts for 1925 give a snapshot of the music and musicians at work: songs and anthems sung by the choir and by soloists dominate, but there were plainly several pianists, a cellist good enough for her own solo and a full school orchestra. James Bates conducted; one of many inspirational music teachers over the years.

Traditional English folk songs seem to have provided the backbone of the concerts: 'Young Richard', 'Dashing away with a smoothing iron', 'The Farmers' Song', interspersed with recitations and the occasional 'pianoforte' piece. Reverend Mother Roantree's feast day was celebrated with

Productions from the 1930s

two concerts (blues and browns) 'consisting entirely of choral singing and recitations, mostly humorous'.

Ena Tighe, a pupil at the school, gave a detailed account of a lecture on sixteenth-century church music given by Father MacDonald and illustrated with examples sung by the choir: 'Pointing out the fact that such music as we spend months in laboriously rehearsing was sung by our forefathers at sight, and for pleasure, Father MacDonald suggested that the musical culture of our days must surely have declined. The choir then rendered most beautifully an "Ave Verum" and a "Salve Regina" by William Byrd, and a motet by Christopher Tye, which was enthusiastically encored.'

'Dramatic Notes' in the 1925 magazine give some flavour of the wide variety of drama performed during a single year. In the Christmas term, Le Cercle de Jeanne

D'Arc performed a 'very successful representation of 'Le Sang qui Prie', presumably in the original French. In the middle term, a group of sixth formers put on a well reviewed production of Sheridan's *The Rivals*, directed by Mother Mostyn, while some of the younger girls performed 'Scenes from *David Copperfield*'. Easter itself was heralded with two performances of Mgr Benson's passion play *The Upper Room*. Finally, the summer term saw what was to have been an open-air production of *A Midsummer Night's Dream* performed indoors because of bad weather. Passion plays and Shakespeare featured regularly in the following years.

One particularly memorable production of *Twelfth Night* was performed at Hillside in 1928. The presence of a pair of identical twins with acting talent enabled Mother Mostyn to present a credible Viola and Sebastian: 'The effect of their resemblance in the recognition scene was really striking.' The weather cooperated for once, enabling the performance to take place on the long terrace. An enthusiastic review praised 'Mary Roantree (whose) keen sense of humour, together with her tall, boyish figure,

The junior choir with their choirmaster 'Daddie' Bates and Miss Gritton, 1930s

fitted her perfectly for the part of Malvolio'. Comfortingly, the reviewer felt that the girl playing Sir Toby Belch 'had evidently not much acquaintance with the effects of liquor'. The review concluded that this was one of the biggest dramatic successes Hillside had yet experienced.

By 1929, the senior and junior choirs were ready to enter a London Music Festival, held in the Central Hall, Westminster. The junior choir won their event and the senior choir, although beaten into second place for their first event, were victorious in the second. As the anonymous author of the report put it: 'We were able to give Reverend Mother the pleasure of seeing us win yet another cup to add to our collection of singing trophies and, better still, of hearing a report which did not point out one single fault, but upheld the reputation of the Hillside choirs for exceptional purity of tone and diction.'

Mother Fehrenbach was just one of the many members of the community who helped to foster a love of music. The 'Music Notes' for 1934, describing the school orchestra, listed Mother Pelly on violin, Mother Fehrenbach on viola,

Above and inset:
A production of
'Hiawatha', 1930s

Opposite: The
'Hiawatha lawn' as
it is today (croquet
lawn and grass
tennis court)

Mother Tombret on cello and Mother Moore on bass; together with the girls, the orchestra numbered sixteen players in all, able to tackle pieces by Handel, Bach and Tchaikovsky.

The regular pattern of services also provided many generations of girls with a deep love for the sacred music which accompanied it. When they first moved up the hill the chapel was in what is now the library, but the opening of the present chapel provided a wonderful new venue for services.

As well as the chapel choir, the girls also had a madrigal choir and a plain chant choir, and took an enthusiastic part in the Gilbert and Sullivan musicals which were a regular feature of school life in the 1930s. Miss Gritton founded a popular Music Club which met weekly to hear talks on lives of the great musicians, listening to records and studying the monthly *Young Musician*. Later they were allowed to 'listen to the weekly concerts on Saturday mornings, so we grouped ourselves round the radiogram in the hall, occupied ourselves with mending, sewing or knitting, and enjoyed half an hour's good music'. Miss Gritton was joined during the war years by Dr Wardale, whose hand-written arrangements and Mass settings, which he composed for the choir, still survive.

Dance was another of the performing arts enthusiastically pursued then as now. Greek dancing and ballroom dancing were both popular, and some of the boarders from Ireland brought their national dance with them. In 1932, for example, a fundraising concert for the building fund included a performance of Irish dancing, while the old girls' garden fete for the same year included both country dancing and a 'Greek ballet' called 'The Sun Fairy'. The

following year, Miss Gritton devised a highly successful pageant, 'Hiawatha', based on the poem by Longfellow. Miss Gritton was responsible for the singing and orchestral accompaniment, while the rest of the staff and girls threw themselves into making props and costumes. The performance took place on the lawn below the house towards Farnborough Road and proved so popular that it was repeated the following year, and then revived at intervals over succeeding decades. Generations of girls knew that area of the grounds as the 'Hiawatha lawn'.

More traditional drama continued to be a popular pastime for both the day girls and boarders. In the school year 1934–5 the plays on offer included *Paddy the Next Best Thing*, *The Immortal Lady*, *The Lady with a Lamp*, *Alison's Lad*, *The Wonderful Tourist*, *The Lost Wig* and *The Pied Piper*. On top of this, the Browns' Dramatic Society (the day girls) put on a separate and almost equally extensive programme. The boarders, of course, had more time available together for rehearsals, but sometimes this could be cut short. A cryptic reference to 'early bed' on a 'good many' evenings suggests that discipline came before artistic endeavour.

Nor was the school afraid to try something new on occasion. The golden jubilee year of 1938–9 saw an

Miss Gritton was my piano teacher who inspired and encouraged in a magical and unforgettable way and I can never forget her influence on my life; and Dr Joseph Wardale, also an exciting and inspiring musician who developed amazing choir work in the school and instilled an everlasting love of music.

Katrina Thompson (Tinkie Gleadell)

the audience sitting near the chapel (now the library) and the orchestra, if any, in the grand salon. It was partly to provide a better performance and meeting space that Mother Roantree planned the Jubilee Wing at the end of the 1930s, which included a large school hall complete with a stage and, eventually, curtains. During the war years the drama and music went on, but the hall had to double as a sports area and a recreation space for the boarders as well. Films were sometimes shown on Sunday evenings, but the acoustics were not always good: 'We enjoyed a film, *The Great Mr Handel*. Unfortunately the voices tended to echo round the hall, so the sound was rather indistinct.'

Early in 1942 the school choir reached a wider audience than usual, when the BBC arrived to record a 'First Friday' Catholic service. After a quick run-through on the day of the service, Friday 5 February, the live broadcast opened with 'Brother James' Air'. The Mass itself was celebrated in Latin, of course, and included a setting of 'Ave Maria' composed by Dr Wardale, the choirmaster. The Reverend John Murray SJ preached an impressive – and fairly lengthy – sermon and concluded by giving the blessing in English. It was to be the first of several such broadcasts over the coming years – and the BBC again came to the school in 2012 to record *Any Questions*, with David Dimbleby in the chair, Cristina Odone on the panel and old girl Victoria Wakeley producing.

ambitious production of TS Eliot's verse play *Murder in the Cathedral*, only three years after its first performance. An enthusiastic review by Father D Boyle began, 'Nobody who had not seen it could have believed that schoolgirls could give so understanding and so moving a performance.' He singled out particular praise for the central character: 'Whoever is bold enough to undertake the part of Becket must either be very good or must fail utterly. Pamela Bruce was a great deal more than very good. From the moment of her first entry to the fall of the curtain she upheld and dominated the whole play, and she held the audience spellbound.' He concluded his review by asserting 'a school that can produce and enjoy a performance of this kind can obviously boast a strong artistic tradition'.

In the early days of their residence in Farnborough Hill, performances had to take place in the lower gallery, with

The 1950s opened with high hopes for the future, and the easing of petrol rationing meant that the girls could enjoy several concerts in Reading, Camberley and elsewhere. Within school, the liturgical calendar gave the chapel choir plenty to do, while the Gilbert and Sullivan tradition (*The Pirates of Penzance* in 1950) went on. The orchestra, though upheld by the continued presence of Mother Moore, Mother Fehrenbach and Mother Bickford, struggled to recruit new members, and put out a plea for girls to 'turn their attention from the all too popular solo performance on the piano to the more stimulating enjoyment of playing in an orchestra'. Interestingly, apart from one pianist, the entire orchestra consisted of string instruments; the days of the ubiquitous flute had yet to come.

When not contributing to Gilbert and Sullivan, the actors of the school found plenty of scope for their talents as the new decade progressed. Shaw's *St Joan* and *Charley's Aunt* appeared in the same year, 1951, which gives some indication of the range they were prepared to tackle. The Community Feast Day play, put on by the Sixth Form, was

The first wartime production of a Gilbert and Sullivan musical was *The Mikado*. As the magazine for 1943–4 noted, staging a musical meant that 'they had, on the one hand to maintain the reputation for singing already gained by the school in two broadcasts, and on the other hand to equal the dramatic achievements of earlier productions like "Hiawatha" and *Murder in the Cathedral*.' Happily, *The Mikado* was a success, with acting, singing, costumes and scenery coming in for praise. *Iolanthe* followed the next year, and Gilbert and Sullivan continued to dominate school musical productions for decades to come.

In 1946, on St Patrick's Day, the new, albeit second-hand, pipe organ was used for the first time. The organ was officially blessed on Ascension Thursday by Bishop King and thereafter was in frequent use, not least because of the great number of big feast days in the summer term. By now the members of the choir were veteran broadcasters and managed to fit in another programme, this time for Children's Hour, in the midst of the Higher and School Certificate examinations. The school continued to encourage girls to pursue music and provided practice rooms, but since these were in the cellars underneath what is now the main staff room, they were scarcely inviting or inspiring.

Cast members from *The Pirates of Penzance*, 1950

The Tumbler of Notre Dame, while the juniors put on The Twelve Brothers and the prefects' Christmas pantomime was Bubble and Squeak. Mother Bickford, with experience of teaching in South America behind her, organised a Spanish fiesta the next spring, including short dramatic sketches performed in Spanish.

Moving on from their broadcasts for the BBC, the school choir made a tape recording of the 'Caro Cibus' by Mendelssohn, arranged by Dr Wardale, which was played at the Religious Vocations Exhibition in Olympia in London. Several decades later the senior choir, under the direction of Karen Kershaw (now Phillips), made a vinyl record of some of their repertoire, which is still fondly remembered by the girls who took part. The cover photo included Mrs Kershaw and music teacher Jill Abbott wearing the same uniform as the girls and blending in remarkably well.

Miss Gritton died in February 1959, after teaching at the school for twenty-nine years. She was recruited in 1927 by Mr Bates, the choirmaster, as an accompanist, and took over the running of the choir on his retirement in 1931 until failing health forced her to retire in 1956. In addition to masterminding the productions of 'Hiawatha', she ran the choirs, played percussion in the orchestra and provided background music for many of the school productions. She was one of a number of inspirational teachers who helped

to foster the school's tradition of music-making in all its forms. Dr Wardale, who had joined her in running the choir during the war years, carried on until 1966.

The previous year Ann Fosh, the head girl, had recorded the excitement of the boarders at being allowed to watch the Beatles 'several times during the year'. A growing disquiet on the part of the community at the influence of popular music led the headmistress, Mother Alexander, to limit the number of evenings girls were allowed to listen to records. In response, some of the boarders established a pop group and began producing their own. Mother Alexander's use of quotation marks when writing about their 'music' indicates exactly what she thought of it.

Above: Karen Phillips conducting the choral concert, 2011

Below left: Vinyl record with Mrs Kershaw and Mrs Abbott in school uniform, 1980

Below: The Senior Choir have released three professionally produced CDs – this one in 2005

Juliet Aubrey, Raquel Cassidy and Rose Keegan

With such a long tradition of drama in its history, it is not surprising that Farnborough Hill has produced a fair number of actresses who have gone on to successful professional careers. Juliet Aubrey remembered how the school helped to nurture her talent: 'Early on I enrolled in drama classes with Mrs Walters. I relished every minute and remember vividly standing behind the door waiting to enter to begin a scene: the nerves, the excitement, the encouragement, the pure love of pretending to be someone else. I can see the room, see Mrs Walters sitting there in her chair, see the sunlight streaming in. We all did the Guildhall/LAMDA exams. It was my sister Sian, though, who really shone in the Walters' school plays: her Freddie in *My Fair Lady* was absolutely stunning. I think that witnessing Sian's brilliance and love of acting inspired me to do it too, and it was definitely at Farnborough Hill that my love for it was awakened and nourished. I am grateful to Mrs Walters for encouraging me from such an early age.' Juliet also fondly remembered music at the school: 'We had an exciting teacher, Mrs Kershaw, and sang our hearts out, contentedly bashing our glockenspiels and xylophones. I was in the choir too, which was a great opportunity to giggle with my friends and sing as loudly as was considered decent and respectful in the chapel. The piano cells (in the cellars) were a labyrinth, with various levels of skill emanating from the walls. There must have been at least twenty pianos down there, available for any girl to play at any time during break.' After leaving Farnborough Hill, Juliet went on to study at King's College, London, and the Central School of Speech and Drama. In a career spanning more than twenty years, she has appeared in the films *Iris, The Constant Gardener, Still Crazy, Welcome to Sarajevo;* the National Theatre's production of *Ivanov* by Chekhov; and television productions of *Middlemarch, The Mayor of Casterbridge, Primeval, Bertie and Elizabeth* and *The White Queen*, among others, earning a BAFTA Best Actress award for her portrayal of Dorothea in *Middlemarch* and a Golden Globe nomination along the way.

Some years later, Raquel Cassidy joined the school; a contemporary remembered her 'on stage in black leathers being Herod. She was fantastic!' In her acting career she may have drawn on her experiences at school when playing the role of Susan Gately in the highly successful television series *Teachers*. More recently, a world-wide television audience saw her in *Downton Abbey* as the lady's maid Baxter, a victim of the bullying valet Thomas.

Rose Keegan, who was three years younger than Raquel, remembered her younger self at Farnborough Hill as 'full of enthusiasm and cheerful but lazy... When I first arrived, I played a wise old man with important news to

Juliet Aubrey

tell in a class Nativity play, and as I had plaits I stuck them together with Sellotape around my chin. I thought it was a very good beard, but when I made my entrance I could see most of the nuns who were watching, and some teachers, unable to stop laughing at me.' Rose went on to the Central School of Speech and Drama and since then has appeared in such varied films as *Thunderbirds, Match Point* and *Magicians,* and television shows such as *Lilies, Hearts and Bones* and *Gimme, Gimme, Gimme,* as well as in theatre.

All three remember their days at school fondly. Rose Keegan wrote: 'Farnborough Hill was an anchor. It was a safe place to be, and to sometimes push against and question. I was always listened to and encouraged to think things through and allowed to be an individual.' Raquel Cassidy recalled the influence of teachers like Mrs Berry when she was interviewed about her own school experiences during *Teachers*, though she admitted that the fictional staff room bore little resemblance to the one she remembered. For her part, Juliet Aubrey wrote, 'I loved Farnborough Hill from the minute I arrived there. We were kind of naughty, I suppose, but it was an innocent naughtiness, more following our sense of fun and adventure, and the nuns allowed that sense to flourish. Independence, invention and free thought were encouraged.' This is echoed by Rose Keegan who concluded, 'Farnborough Hill taught us to take personal responsibility, to be honest and truthful, with yourself and others, and to do the right thing, and not be swayed by influences that were not true.'

Rose Keegan

Raquel Cassidy

Just A Note

Writing in the school magazine of 1993, Jill Abbott set out to answer the question 'why it began'. Its origins lay in her own early life when she discovered how music could reach out to the handicapped. Her mother worked in a school for the deaf and Mrs Abbott, who played the organ in the local church, noticed how the deaf children loved feeling the music through its vibrations. Later, when asked to play for a party of the mentally handicapped, she found herself surrounded by 'an enthusiastic group of men, all talking excitedly, touching my hands as I played and stroking my long hair'. After her initial surprise she realised that 'music could break through any barriers'. Mrs Abbott put this insight into practice at Farnborough Hill by establishing Just A Note as a biweekly informal musical ensemble who once a month welcomed students from a special school, Coppers School in Fleet, to make music. They also regularly carried their talents out into the community, performing in hospitals, for organisations such as the Stroke Club and in retirement homes. Over the years they raised thousands of pounds for such causes as the Guide Dog Association and the Red Cross. It was partly to play for the Red Cross that they undertook several tours to Switzerland, as well as going on pilgrimage to Walsingham and Lourdes.

Just A Note and friends, 1998/9

By this time, the talent competition was a well established annual event, organised by two of the houses. Entries included ballet, songs, gymnastic displays, short plays and piano solos. The Sixth Form prefects contributed a skit about the Trojan War, which climaxed when twenty of them appeared from the wooden vaulting horse which they had borrowed from the gym. Helen Griffiths remembered that 'the scope allowed for satire was remarkable, with nuns frequently lending their veils for the purpose of utterly irreverent comic impersonations'.

As well as performing their own plays and musicals, the girls were taken to a good many professional productions, both in Farnham and London. One outing was to *The Merchant of Venice* at the Haymarket Theatre, with Sir Ralph Richardson as Shylock, and a group of sixth formers went to see Shaw's controversial *Black Girl in Search of God*. However, there does not seem to have been anything *avant garde* about the staging of *My Fair Lady* in 1969, in place of the traditional Gilbert and Sullivan. This enlargement of the repertoire was popular, but the play presented the usual challenges of providing convincing actors to take the male roles. Sheila Green, who played Higgins, was admired for 'clear enunciation', though the reviewer also noted that 'the make-up and pitch of her voice could not disguise her youth'. A decade later the same musical had Freddie being played by Sian Aubrey, the older sister of Juliet, at that time relegated to the part of a street urchin but later to become a professional actress with a string of leading roles in film, television and theatre. From then on, Gilbert and Sullivan took a back seat as the school experimented with *The Boyfriend*, *Animal Farm* and *The Sound of Music* among many others.

Drama was by this time in the hands of the redoubtable Joan Walters, remembered fondly by generations of girls for her many and varied productions. About this time Mrs Walters revived the tradition of 'choral speaking' and successfully entered teams in the

Farnborough Hill goes to Hollywood

In June 1990 the head of drama, Joan Walters, was startled to receive a phone call from Walt Disney Films. 'We are looking for 100 girls to take part in the sequel to *Three Men and a Baby*, to be called *Three Men and a Little Lady*' she was told. Not surprisingly, a great many girls wanted to take part; selection was based, somewhat bizarrely, on whether they could fit into the costumes which had already been created for the fictional 'Pileforth Academy'. The chosen 100 set out on 11 July for Douai Abbey where their scenes were to be filmed. The plot concerned the efforts of the English grandmother of Mary, the 'little lady', to have her enrolled in a very strict English boarding school. Inevitably the plot pandered to American prejudices about the joyless life of English schoolgirls; though ironically, the greatest challenge that the selected girls faced was looking sufficiently miserable on camera. The film starred Tom Selleck and Steve Guttenberg with whom the girls were suitably star-struck.

Jo Oliver and Clare Byrne, two members of the Upper Sixth who took part, described the experience in breathless detail: 'Turn over... sound running... roll 180... take 15... quiet on the set... action! The fifteenth time of facing a plate of cold fish and mushy peas and at the same time sitting rigidly upright and biting our tongues to keep ourselves from collapsing in a fit of giggles.

'We have now been here at Douai Abbey, one of the locations used, since 8.15am. The first scene we were needed for was the dining room scene. We were told that our purpose in this film was to give the impression to the school's visitors, Peter and Michael, played by Tom Selleck and Steve Guttenberg, that this was not the kind of place to which they would like to send Mary. This was extremely difficult for the majority of us! Eventually, however, after threats of more servings of cold fish, we got it right – it only took two hours and seventeen takes!

'We then waited to be called for the next scene. We were taken to the corridor in which it was to be shot and told what we were expected to do: to walk in pairs precisely down a corridor past the actors on the opposite side of the corridor without smiling or acknowledging their presence. In theory this sounds easy! But imagine not smiling when Steve Guttenberg smiles at you and says something funny!' Two of the accompanying teachers were also chosen as extras; Mrs Holdaway and Mrs Abbott were transformed for the occasion into 'stiff school-ma'ams in conformity with the American image of the English school teacher'.

In 1998, HRH Prince Edward used Farnborough Hill as a backdrop for his film about the friendship between Queen Victoria and Empress Eugenie. Two members of staff, Claire Hamilton and Anne Downes, played the queens, though fortunately only without sound since, as Miss Downes put it, 'I don't think the world is ready for a Queen Victoria with an Irish accent.'

Above: Farnborough Hill girls have difficulty looking miserable for the camera in *Three Men and a Little Lady* in this montage of images

Below: Prince Edward with Anne Downes and Claire Hamilton

Wimbledon Music Festival. In 1975, she also entered public speaking teams for the English Speaking Union and the Knights of St Columba Public Speaking Competition, winning second place in the latter. Mrs

Winch-Johnson's highly successful teams thirty years later are part of a long tradition.

On 31 May 1979 the distinguished actress Margaret Rawlings gave the school a preview of her one-woman production of *Empress Eugenie* prior to two public performances held in the school hall. Claire, Morag and Penelope Allison reported that 'It was an eerie sensation to see an elderly, faded, black-clad figure glide silently and gracefully across the stage in the house where her spirit still pervades the glass and marble decor. One had the strange feeling of experiencing more than one royal presence.'

In the late 1970s O level drama was introduced, for which twenty girls devised a practical dramatic piece called 'The House on the Hill' based on Mother Mostyn's book. From then on, drama became a recognised option for the examination years, and has remained popular ever since. By 1986 A level theatre studies had been added to the curriculum, and expressive forms of dance gained new impetus with the arrival in 1986 of Yvonne Cullen to teach jazz dance as well as drama.

As the 1983 magazine reported, the effect of parish reorganisation in Farnborough meant the disappearance of the monthly sung Mass in chapel on Sunday. However, the chapel choir continued to rehearse regularly for services inside school, and outside school took part in one of the pre-Christmas carol concerts in London. The previous year they had joined the London Oriana Choir, the English Baroque Choir and English Renaissance Players in two concerts in the Royal Albert Hall. Mrs Abbott was, by this time, well established as a member of the music department, and with her 'Just a Note' group helped to provide the girls with plenty of opportunities to make music.

Drama was not all home produced, of course. Elizabeth McDonald, a well loved member of the English department, produced an entertaining account of taking parties of girls to the theatre, to workshops and to Stratford itself: 'Shall we take all the Fifth Year to Stratford to see *Romeo and Juliet*? My heart sinks at the thought of 100 green-striped blazers rushing into half-timbered birthplaces in search not of the real Shakespeare but Crunchie bars.' Madeleine Howard remembers a trip to see Peter O'Toole's *Macbeth* in 1980 with Mrs Macdonald: 'The play had been heavily slated in the press so as we settled ourselves in our seats in "the gods" we were intrigued to find that from our high vantage point we were able to see behind the scenes to the side of the stage where a bottle stood on a table from which Peter O'Toole frequently took a swig during the performance. Progressively he seemed to forget his lines so that at several points in the

play the "Farnborough Hill Chorus" pelted out the texts learned by rote. Needless to say Mrs McDonald remonstrated, but we thoroughly enjoyed the "Scottish play".'

Drama might not seem to be a competitive sport on a par with netball and hockey, but in the 1980s and 1990s the school entered a number of local performing arts festivals and did commendably well in such fields as verse speaking, choral speaking and Bible reading as well as more conventional offerings such as group drama. On Mrs Walters' retirement in the early 1990s, although these skills were still much in evidence the focus shifted away from external competition to internal school productions.

1992 saw the arrival of Lynette Newman as head of music. From the first, she worked well with Mrs Abbott, collaborating with her on a range of musical activities. Staff, parents and girls joined to perform Haydn's *Nelson Mass* in her first year, and the first informal concert took place in the school hall, providing a chance for individuals and small groups to perform for an audience of family and friends. Under Mrs Newman's stern yet kindly gaze, the school choir grew and included members of staff for the first time. The ambitious choral concerts became a regular part of the school calendar, while the drama department busied itself with more 'straight' dramas.

Lynette Newman accompanying girls in the Grand Salon

Lady Precious Stream, 1996

then a popular police drama, and with the distinction of having appeared in *Dr Who* as well. He began his directing career with an Inuit creation story, *Whale,* and followed it up the following year with *Lady Precious Stream*, thus firmly taking the settings and costumes for the plays out of the British Isles for the first time in years. His choice of *The Caucasian Chalk Circle* was more controversial, with one governor reputedly unhappy about the fact that it was written by a Marxist and asking plaintively why they could not go back to the repertoire of Gilbert and Sullivan. *The Tempest* and *Animal Farm* were more mainstream productions, though with memorably inventive costumes and staging.

Above: A level students in John Godber's *Shakers*, 2008

Below: Lower Sixth AS candidates in Caryl Churchill's *Fen*, 2010

Mrs Walters retired from Farnborough Hill in 1994 after twenty-seven years, during which she trained thousands of girls, directed countless productions and inspired many with her enthusiasm and flair. Steve Morley, her replacement, arrived fresh from a regular role in *The Bill*,

Lizzie Rhodes

One of the Fifth Form music students, Elizabeth Rhodes, composed a Latin setting for the Mass which she named 'Ferneberge' after the Domesday name for Farnborough. The choir performed it for a school Mass, and the story of its composition was taken up by the local and national press and Radio Leicester. The following year, while studying music at A level, Lizzie followed it up with an English Mass setting which is still used for school Masses nearly twenty years later.

Early in his time as head of drama, Mr Morley persuaded the headmistress to allow him to convert the Princess' Studio into a small theatre by painting it black, providing black-out blinds and installing a lighting booth. This not only gave better facilities for drama teaching but provided a venue for small, informal performances such as the popular 'Lunchbox Theatre' series, with examination classes and drama clubs performing for their fellow students. In place of the large-scale Christmas shows organised by Mrs Walters, Mr Morley and the music department collaborated on a new type of Christmas entertainment, the Christmas Celebration, which combined short drama sketches and choral speaking with seasonal music from the full range of music groups in the school.

Music too was changing – and expanding. The first Informal Music evening had been so successful that it had had to split into two, junior and senior, on different nights. Mrs Newman reported that the junior choir numbered fifty members in 1996, and the orchestra had expanded to forty. The senior choir was also large, by now reinforced by several enthusiastic teachers who joined the girls in their lunchtime rehearsals and came in for their fair share of 'Newman frowns'. As before, one of their main functions was to provide the music for services in the chapel, but now with prize giving reinstated, there was more scope for secular music as well. Such was Mrs Newman's acute ear that, after hearing an unusual descant added to a familiar hymn at the funeral of Diana, Princess of Wales, she promptly wrote it down and taught it to the choir the following week. When one of the Sisters in Lafosse died

The Boyfriend, 2012. The set was one of many designed by Rosie Byrne (formerly Pocock), who has been head of art since 1988. The entire art department along with many other teachers from a wide range of departments pool their collective talents each year in order to assist the music and drama departments by designing and making costumes, providing make-up and creating realistic props.

Choir tour to Barcelona, 2011

unexpectedly, it was discovered that she had asked for Handel's *Hallelujah Chorus* at her funeral; Mrs Newman not only managed to produce an arrangement for female voices in a matter of days, but had trained the choir to sing it by the time the funeral took place at the end of the week.

In 2001 Mrs Newman decided to return to her former occupation of piano teaching and her place was taken by Karen Kershaw (now Phillips). Under her lively direction, old traditions like the Choral Concert and Christmas Celebration were maintained and new ones added. The senior chamber choir were given the opportunity to sing at Saturday evening Mass in Westminster Cathedral and proved so successful that this has become a regular booking; they have also sung Evensong at Salisbury Cathedral on a number of occasions. In 2005, the first choir tour to Italy took place. Girls and staff sang in a range of venues in and around Venice, ranging from an open-air chapel in a campsite to St Mark's Cathedral. The tours have become bi-annual events, with subsequent groups going to Lake Garda, Spain and Tuscany.

In the same year, Mr Morley too moved on and was succeeded by Davina Franzoni (later Mrs Robinson). One of her early productions was her own version of a medieval mystery play, performed partly in the school hall and partly in the chapel. It was inspired by a trip the entire school made to the open-air pageant of 'The Life of Christ' at Wintershall to celebrate the millennium, and made a dramatic start to her time at the school. Since then there has been an alternation of musicals, in collaboration with the music department, and 'straight' drama, albeit sometimes with incidental music, as with *The Canterbury Riders*.

The conversion of the former gymnasium in 2009 into a theatre with retractable seating and a giant, pull-down screen has brought more scope to school drama. *Epsom Downs* used the new space to memorable effect, with the downs being represented by a huge expanse of artificial grass merging into a back-projection of a racecourse. Drama remains a popular examination option and this new performance space has eased the pressure on the school hall as a teaching venue.

Throughout the school's history, performance has been very important both within the curriculum and as a stimulating activity open to everyone. As with sport, a combination of talented girls and inspirational teachers has played a major role in remaining true to the original vision of the founding Sisters in 'educating the whole person'.

A selection of recent artwork, including painting, ceramics, textiles and photography

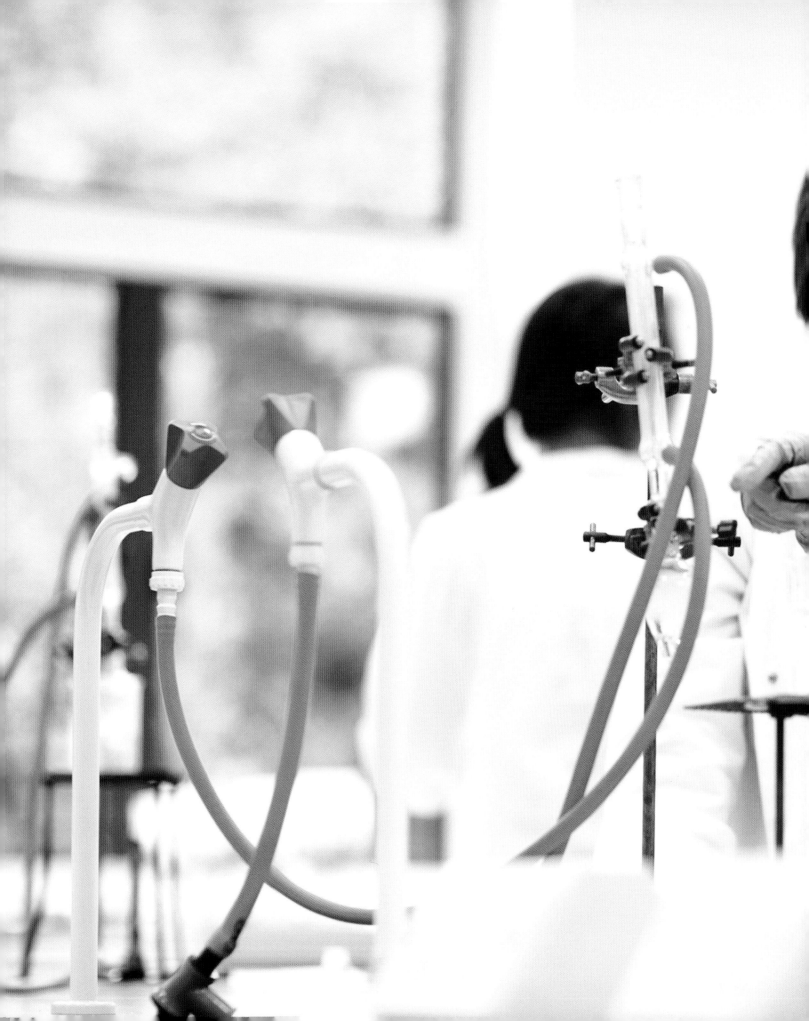

3

Into the present

The 1960s: the shock of the new

As the 1950s drew to a close, the school found itself with a new headmistress. Mother Hogan had succeeded Mother Horan earlier in the decade, but now ill health forced her to step down and her place was taken by a former pupil, Rosemary Alexander. From Farnborough Hill, Rosemary had gone to Trinity College, Dublin, and then joined the Order. Mother Alexander proved to be an inspirational leader who oversaw the further expansion of the school and experimented with modern ideas such as mixed ability teaching. During her tenure a whole new wing was added, including the longed-for gymnasium, and the school expanded from two-form entry to three. As Ann Berry (Tristram), a pupil at the school during the 1960s recalls, 'Mother Alexander took it from being a school for educating young ladies to a school providing education for girls.' The number of O levels considered appropriate went up from five to seven or more in the space of just a few years.

In her Headmistress's Report for 1963, Mother Alexander explained the thinking behind this radical new idea of mixed ability teaching: 'At the age of eleven, on the results of the Common Entrance Examination, a girl was placed in either IA or Form I, the Form Is being considered the somewhat slower of the two streams. Despite some limited movement between the two as they moved up the

The 1960s
block

Photo taken in the community room, now M1. Left to right, Sister Byrne, Sister Butterley, Sister McCormack, Mother Alexander, Sister Cahill, Sister Dawson, Sister O'Looney, Sister Bourne. Both Sister Dawson and Sister McCormack later became headmistress

school, the result was that too many girls found themselves typecast for life at the age of eleven.' By 1959 both staff and girls were beginning to suffer some hardship from what could be called a 'plain' complex – 'those plain IIIs, we'll never do anything with them' or 'we're the plain form, we can't do it'. So that September, the girls returned to find their classes re-christened: IA and IAlpha. The bright, not so bright and average were equally distributed between the As and the Alphas, the idea being that the not so bright girls would be encouraged by seeing the achievements and standards of the brighter ones, and the latter would get on anyway and profit considerably in character by not always being the centre of attention. French, Latin and mathematics were exempted from this arrangement and continued to be taught by ability.

By 1963 she felt able to report on the success of the scheme: 'Standards of attainment rose – girls from the middle of a "plain" form began coming near the top of the list in their A or Alpha form and the bright ones still did well.' She concluded by noting how this placed Farnborough Hill at the forefront of current educational thinking: 'I am pleased to see that the educational press has recently endorsed these ideas.'

Another challenge faced by the new headmistress was what to do about the increased numbers qualifying for admission. After discussion, the decision was made to add a third form – Omega – to the two existing ones. The extra class was initially installed in the ever-versatile huts, but this could only be a temporary measure. The increasing popularity of science also meant that new laboratories for chemistry and biology were urgently required. During the 1950s, girls had had to use laboratories in St Anne's, near the swimming pool. Now a large new block was planned, which would provide 'chemistry and biology laboratories, an art room, three classrooms, a staff cloakroom, a day girls'

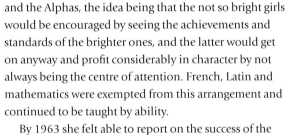

Staff v prefects hockey match, with Mother Alexander, 1961

cloakroom, a gym and changing room and a dormitory'. As Mother Alexander explained, 'That still leaves us without common rooms for the boarders, a needlework room, a kitchen large enough for a full-sized class for O level, a working room for the staff and adequate teaching space for three streams, if we have them, and teaching space for such subjects as singing and elocution.'

In her 1963 speech to governors and parents, Mother Alexander outlined the curriculum followed by girls at the school. For the first three years, the three parallel forms studied a common curriculum, followed by 'the first element of choice: physics and chemistry for those reasonably good at mathematics; an additional modern language – Spanish, German or Italian; Greek; or O level courses in cookery and needlework. Once the choices are made the girls automatically group themselves for the coming two years prior to the O level examinations. Divisions in French, mathematics and Latin still run simultaneously on the timetable so that continuity and interchange are possible.' She also noted that the 'academic Sixth Form has been steadily increasing in size and that in September over thirty will be going into the various academic groups of the first year Sixth, and twenty into the second year. As far as I can see, these numbers will be increased by between ten and twenty in 1964.'

Those less academically inclined could take a one year general course in which the students could study for an A level in English literature or a domestic science subject while spending the rest of their time in 'doctrine, British institutions, a modern language, current events, art and music appreciation and physical education'. Both sets of students met for study and discussion in their general subjects, 'a practice you will have seen advocated recently in the national press'.

The 1963 magazine carries a photograph of the newly dug foundations of the new wing. Building work began in March that year, with bulldozers levelling out the few remaining yards of hilltop and enlarging the area by building up soil on the slope overlooking St Anne's, into which forty-foot piles were driven to take the weight of the new building. The west side of the new quadrangle was, and is, taken up with science laboratories, but the room which is now the biology lab was designed as an art room with a very large, north-facing window jutting out over the

The fundraising appeal for the new block

hillside. Between the two new labs were a preparation room and a photographic dark room. On the east side was the main entrance between cloakrooms (one of which is now Geography Room 1) and a changing area with washroom. Next to the new art room were three classrooms, now converted into two physics laboratories.

Nearly twenty-five years after losing a school gymnasium in the move from Hillside College, the school finally had a new one, on the fourth side of the new quadrangle. This is now the Theatre on the Hill. Above it, where the maths department is now centred, were a well equipped needle-work room, a lecture theatre and other teaching rooms for the Sixth Form, together with a reading room and study. The top floor was given over to sleeping quarters. Mother Mostyn describes it as quite luxurious: 'This new dormitory, decorated in pastel shades and floored with lino-tiles of soft green, is made over to fourth and fifth formers. There are two staff bedrooms and the rest of the space contains built-in cubicles, each fitted with a wardrobe, drawers and

Views of the new block, mid 1960s, including, *top left*, the lecture theatre (now Room 22); *above*, gymnasium (now Theatre on the Hill); and *left*, dormitory cubicles (now food technology)

shelves for a girl's books and ornaments, with a reading light over each bed. There is a fitted washroom with bathrooms and toilets. The cubicles have large windows with a far-reaching view, one side overlooking the rose-tiled courtyard which is equipped with benches and large concrete plant-bowls; here the girls collect for their mid-morning break.' Later generations of Farnborough Hill girls, recalling the bleak and unlovely space which was the central courtyard, may struggle to reconcile their memory of it with this description.

Paying for such a large extension was, as with earlier building projects, a matter of fundraising. Parents, old girls and other well-wishers all contributed to the building fund. Ann Fosh, the head girl that year, raised £10 towards the

building fund by levying a penny fine for talking on the chapel corridor. Her report in the magazine on this initiative also included a passing reference to 'watching' a new band – the Beatles. That verb 'to watch' incidentally reveals the presence of a television at the school; a decade earlier, the headmistress had rented a television to enable the Sisters and boarders to watch the Coronation, but now the school had a set of its own – still black and white, of course – on which they could keep abreast of current events including, in November 1963, the assassination of President Kennedy.

School trips abroad were now becoming more frequent. In April 1963 a party of nine Third Form girls and several nuns, plus Mr Newsham, the driver, set off on a trip to

A typing class, *left*, and dressmaking class, *below*, 1960s

France, and the following year members of the Fourth, Fifth and Lower Sixth went on a two-week trip to Rome with Mother Rennie, Madame and Miss Florence, managing to take in Pompeii as well as Rome itself.

Life was certainly not 'stopped and preserved in the past' at Farnborough Hill, but the Headmistress's Report for 1964 revealed a growing disquiet at the influence of 'the affluent society', as she termed it, on the school. New hair styles, not for the last time, were causing problems: 'We waste a great deal of time and energy in admonishing ill-groomed girls… to keep their lanky locks under control and

Memories of the 1963 trip to France

We drove to Southampton in the school minibus and suffered a broken windscreen on the way. We travelled with the girls in the front seat holding cardboard up to the missing window. At Southampton, the van was lifted onto the ship (no roll-on roll-off!) and an AA man travelled on the ferry to fit a new windscreen overnight. We visited several convents in Normandy and were all much taken with the idea that boarders in France had curtained cubicles – no open dormitories. In one convent we horrified our

French hosts by a girl saying 'Je suis plein' when offered more food; this is apparently French slang for 'I am pregnant'. I have an abiding memory of the nuns coming down a long flight of open steps at Mont San Michel with their cloaks billowing out in the wind so they looked like galleons in full black sail. We wore uniform throughout the trip, including our day in Paris at the end, and I remember travelling on very crowded metro trains and getting split up.

Claire Scargill (Nicholson)

The Duke of Edinburgh's Award

A graphic illustration of the changes in society that have taken place over the past fifty years comes by comparing the topics covered by the Duke of Edinburgh's Award in 1964 with those of 2014. Then there were four main areas of activity: 'Design for Living', 'Interests', 'Adventure' and 'Service'. The last two form the backbone of most Duke of Edinburgh activities now, but fifty years ago the emphasis at Farnborough Hill was on more ladylike pursuits. Under 'Design for Living' they could study 'grooming and poise', with special reference to make-up and hairstyles; clothes; courtesy; education and budgeting; setting up and running a home. 'Interests' for girls included archery, aquarium keeping, drama, hamster keeping, Scottish country dancing and wild flower collecting. 'Adventure' was intended to 'widen the horizons of each girl and to encourage initiative' while the list of suggested activities for service included 'home nursing, life saving, helping the deaf and dumb or blind, the care of animals or teaching in Sunday School'.

DofE Needlework, 1970s

look less like the popular image of whatever the teenage idol is at the moment. Apart from anything else, it does not go with the school uniform.'

Part of the problem seemed to be the boarders' leisure time. She recorded how she had at first pursued a tolerant line when viewing their preference for 'pop records and the latest form of twist or shake', defending them to critical parents with the retort 'they must let off steam sometimes; they can't be organised all the time'. However, further enquiry convinced her that more formal activities needed to be provided, particularly at weekends when, apart from

Mass on Sunday, the girls had mostly been left to make their own amusements. But when she discovered that these amusements were almost entirely listening to popular music, she decided that something had to be done. The new regime indicated that 'the gramophone for pop records is allowed after supper on Wednesdays, for an hour on Saturday afternoons and after lunch on Sundays.' At other times more traditional pursuits were encouraged: board games, photography, table tennis, chess and reading. The reaction of the girls was, perhaps predictably, not enthusiastic. A plea went out for parents to send their daughters to school 'with the materials for some sort of hobby', but few bothered to do so, prompting the exasperated headmistress to remark, 'If parents are apathetic and seem hardly to care if their daughters are the pop type, then we in school can do little to raise their standard.' This final phrase speaks volumes for the school's attitude to 'the swinging sixties'.

Popular culture was not the only threat at this time to the traditions of Farnborough Hill. While the school was continuing to grow, the hostility of the Labour government to selective education created a climate of uncertainty. Farnborough Hill had, for a number of years, admitted a certain number of girls from the state sector under the 11+ system. However, it was far from clear that this would continue indefinitely, and in fact it did come to an end a few years later, with schools given the choice of becoming fully independent of government funding or joining the state – and comprehensive – system. This was some years in the future, but even in 1965, the writing was clearly on the wall: 'With all that is being said and written about

reorganisation in education, comprehensive schemes on the one hand and the position of the public schools on the other, I have no doubt that it must have crossed many minds to wonder what the future of schools like this really is. It is a question that no one can answer with assurance. I can only say that we in Farnborough Hill are not living in any fool's paradise. We are well aware of modern trends. As headmistress, I belong to various professional bodies which are all working on this question of reorganisation.' With the benefit of fifty years of hindsight, it is easy to underestimate the challenge that these uncertainties posed to the headmistress and the community at the time. We know that the school survived, thrived and developed, but at the time, whether this would happen must have seemed considerably less clear cut.

Under Mother Alexander's leadership the Sixth Form grew and developed. In 1964 thirty-three girls completed A level courses in the Upper Sixth. Of those, fourteen went on to university including two each to Oxford and Cambridge. Six girls went to teacher training colleges, five were to study nursing and others were to pursue non-degree qualifications in music, physical education, drama and speech therapy. In view of the open discrimination against female students in many fields, and the fact that far fewer places were available to women, especially at Oxbridge, this is a remarkable progression rate. It is clear that the school's policy of preparing girls for careers, not just for motherhood, was well established.

By 1965 Mother Alexander was able to tell parents that thirty-seven fourth formers had started on the Duke of Edinburgh Scheme, although by the end of the school year their numbers had dropped to fifteen. The most popular activities were gymnastics and guitar playing; the limit on pop record listening had led to a number of home-grown

pop groups. The school was also facing increasing competition from the local technical colleges as girls opted to pursue their Sixth Form education in a less tightly restricted environment. In response, she set out her aims: 'To help to equip a girl spiritually, mentally, academically and socially for everyday life in this exacting, but exciting modern world'. As she acknowledged, the recent changes in the wider Catholic Church made catechetics teaching more complicated and challenging than before. However, as one

old girl of the time remembers, 'The greatest catechesis or "teaching" that I ever had was the example during Mass of our nuns at Farnborough Hill… Anyone entering the chapel at that time, regardless of their belief or lack of it, would understand from the example of those Religious that something very sacred was taking place.'

In the 1960s, as in the twenty-first century, the need to keep a balance between modernity and tradition – 'a middle road between the outmoded and the outrageous' – exercised those who led the school. It was clear that society was changing, and becoming less deferential and less unquestioning in its attitudes. And while Farnborough Hill remained largely insulated from the more extreme social changes taking place, some of the tensions of the time are evident in the recollections of old girls of the period. A recurring theme is the ongoing coolness between day girls and boarders. Ann Berry (Tristram) remembers an indignant delegation of boarders going to see the headmistress when she, a day girl, was made games captain – formerly a boarder's privilege. Some of the difficulty may have been territorial. Farnborough Hill, after all, was home to the boarders but only a place of study to the day girls, and the boarders may have felt that they had a much stronger association with the place. However, the petty snobberies of the time are likely to have been more to blame. Boarders were largely the children of diplomats or high ranking military officers who were posted overseas, while day girls, and especially the scholarship girls, were from local families. The nuns were well aware of these tensions and did their best to discourage them.

Memories of Farnborough Hill from Anne Robinson

I chose to go to Farnborough because I loved the striped blazer, which was much jazzier than the one on offer at St Mary's, Ascot. Not the most academic of reasons. But then I had a mother with a capricious view of authority and an entirely unorthodox approach to parenting. In fact, I spent my first year at Yateley Hall, then the prep school, where alas the uniform was a reddish pink smock worn with a white blouse and horrible peter pan collar. Not a good look for a tubby freckled redhead. Even more disappointing, there wasn't a single book to be found in the school library by my heroine Enid Blyton. She was banned. Yet Enid Blyton's tales of exciting boarding school life at St Clare's and Mallory Towers were almost entirely responsible for my begging my parents to send me away to school. That and feeling lonely since my brother had already left for Ampleforth.

No matter, Yateley Hall is and was a beautiful building; a picture postcard example of an eighteenth-century country home in pale red brick. The chapel overlooked a moat, there was a haha separating the drive from the fields beyond and a big enough tree outside the nuns' community room for us to listen and giggle at the gossip going on inside.

From that first year I recall the painful attempts to get the hang of the italic writing taught by the gamine Miss Hickey who had an expected but ferocious temper; the lessons in old-time dancing – I can still do a mean Military Two-Step and Gay Gordons; horse-riding on a Wednesday afternoon; and the endless games of jacks, hopscotch and pick-up sticks at the weekends. But perhaps most of all the magic of living in a house so much grander than my suburban home in the north.

Mother Pelly, the headmistress, had no truck with bad behaviour or idleness or gossip, whereas the Sisters who did the laundry and worked in the kitchen were endlessly tolerant of our high jinks and tales of our families. Looking back, the distinction between the Mothers and Sisters was feudal but those were very different times.

My memories of Farnborough are really random snapshots. I was an unruly pupil, impatient with subjects in which I had no interest (almost everything bar English and history) and on a daily basis unable to grasp the importance of paying attention and benefiting from what I was being taught. I don't recommend this approach but I've often argued that conformity can be a drawback when it comes to the jobs market. And that those of us who, for whatever reason, fail to toe the line and fit in at school are sometimes better suited to the treachery of the work place and adapt more easily to the inequality of adult life.

What teacher inspired me? There's no contest. It was Miss Dorothy Dayus who came every Thursday afternoon to give private drama lessons in one of the smaller parlours. She told me I had a talent to perform and insisted I would easily obtain a scholarship to study drama at Guildhall School of Music where she was one of the principals. Nothing but nothing is as empowering as an early validation of one's strengths. Typically, I ignored her advice.

Elsewhere, and not surprisingly given my attitude, I was mostly a scholastic disaster. This was my fault and not the quality of teaching. I simply refused to get involved. I was also utterly hopeless at art, singing and ballet dancing. As for needlework, despite Mrs Ewing's best efforts, I was still struggling to complete a now grubby pinafore begun in my first term when others in the class had created whole wardrobes of clothes. But I adored spending hours in the library, where there was always a fresh copy of the *Daily Telegraph*. I loved the theatre and movies and books. I first saw the classics *Some Like it Hot* and *The Dam Busters* at school. Winston Churchill's account of the Second World War shown on the BBC and narrated by Richard Burton was set up on a large screen for us to see on six consecutive Sunday evenings.

The summer concert in our time alternated between a Gilbert and Sullivan opera and a play. I was the voice of Bernadette of Lourdes in a production written by Hugh Ross Williamson, the father of a Farnborough Hill pupil – a fantastic experience, even if by the time we were ready to perform to an audience Mother Alexander, the headmistress, declared she could think of no one less suited to playing the part of a future saint.

Mother Alexander arrived in my second year at Farnborough. She replaced Mother Hogan, a kindly and quiet nun but with a wonderful sense of humour. I never see the words 'Christian Dior' without thinking of her. In school assembly she told us he had died the night before and as a mark of respect we should all make sure the hems on our skirts and shorts were properly even.

Mother Alexander was made of much sterner stuff. She was an old girl with a formidable academic reputation and an uncrushable belief in discipline. Mother A did not just require us to have nicely sewn hems, but rather she declared zero tolerance towards individual variations on the school uniform. Among her many other stern dictates, she informed us that at the beginning of each term we must write and thank our families for the holidays and when we arrived home we must write and thank the school for the term.

Thanks, Mother A. It took me decades to get the point. But I am and always have been a very decent writer of thank you letters. I only wish I'd had more use for performing an elegant curtsey – particularly done sideways while carrying a large pile of books. It was obligatory if we passed visitors sitting in the glass parlour as we made our way to the library.

Once a year we endured the school retreat. Silence for a whole two days or was it three? It seemed like a lifetime. Instead of the usual chatter in the refectory somebody was chosen to read to us. Thanks again, Mother A. Nearly always I was that somebody. Trust me, once you've stood on a high chair with your green knickers on show to the whole school and read very boring extracts from a learned book of theology, it is possible to perform live on television to an audience of millions without even blinking.

Ascension Thursday, a holy day of obliga-tion, was marked out for a school expedition. Often this was to the seaside. But one year, imaginatively, we were taken to the Tate and saw the first ever Picasso exhibition. It turned me into a lifelong devotee. Similarly, an English teacher whose name I sadly forget arranged for the Fourth Form to see a matinee performance of *Richard II*, starring Alec Clunes (father of Martin) at the Aldwych. We then had to write a critique. I took a chance with my essay and also described our journey to London and the fun and games on the way back in the coach. My effort was read out. Again I say it: there is no greater incentive for a child than to have their good work acknowledged.

Too nuanced to fit into a questionnaire is the most important thing that Farnborough Hill gave me. It was a sense of self-belief and inner confidence. We were girls from different parts of the world, different backgrounds and different upbringings, thrown together. It naturally and unconsciously widened our knowledge and ability to mix. How could it not? Some came from the Far East, the Caribbean, Africa and North and South America. We would swap the

letters from our parents, and from those I probably learnt more than I did from any geography lesson.

Living for five years in the most exquisite of houses and being schooled in good manners and given the tools to conduct ourselves socially might seem like old-fashioned plus points, but they should not be underestimated. As a woman who has spent a lifetime urging younger women to ignore glass ceilings, I know that the vital ingredient for doing so is confidence.

Few of us, of course, could appreciate the amazing dedication, hard work and devotion of the nuns any more than we could begin to understand the enormous personal sacrifice they had made to serve God. I am delighted to have this chance to say to the Sisters of Christian Education, thank you.

Anne Robinson

Boarding life

Although they shared the same building and, in the case of the younger girls, the same dormitory, the accounts of boarding life given by the Sisters and the boarders themselves differ widely. Photographs of the time show rows of immaculately made beds and carefully regimented girls bent obediently over their homework in the library or entrance hall. Certainly they were carefully supervised at night. Sister McDonnell, who arrived in 1963, remembers that during term time the only privacy she had at night came when she was able to escape to the 'geyser room' (bathroom) for a few minutes after her charges were in bed. Homesick girls could turn to motherly nuns for comfort, but the school also offered considerable scope for mischief, albeit of a fairly innocent kind. Nicky Hall (Turle), writing in her memoir 'From Granny with Love', remembered hiding 'to escape games or lessons that we did not like. When hiding in a cupboard once, I saw through a keyhole one of the more severe nuns advancing fast towards my hiding place with the determination of the Gestapo. It was unnerving. I only had a house mark removed and was promptly sent down two fields to the freezing hockey pitch.' A more sophisticated ruse was to feign illness. One of her

The reality and the ideal: *right*, a cartoon in the school magazine, 1960s, Sister Rennie looking disapproving; and *below*, a study bedroom, 1951

in a state of mortal dread. Barbara Howells (Zamoyska), writing many years later, remembered, 'Our chapel was beautiful and evoked a very special atmosphere. At dusk, with the candles flickering and perhaps the organist practising, it offered such a sense of peace and well-being that I sometimes conjure that image as a tranquillising therapy'.

Nicky Hall (Turle) remembered, despite the vigilance of the nuns, being able to wander around at night and admire the glass ceiling of the quad, while two of her

friends pretended that she had lost her voice and was able to spend an entire day in the infirmary, reading *Lord of the Flies*.

House marks still loomed large as a means of control. Each girl began with 100 and had them deducted for such offences as running in the corridor or answering back. At Assembly each week the headmistress would read out the names and their house marks. 'Nothing filled me with greater terror than our headmistress reading the names of the girls plus their marks. The rest of the nuns were all seated up on the stage, the backdrop of which was black, so all that was visible were the white wimples at various different levels. Worse than this was our headmistress rattling through the 100s, 99s and 98s, but, with a voice expressive of the deepest shock, pausing for excruciating seconds on totals of 95 or lower. Had the nuns been armed with live ammunition, I could not, in my first term, have been in more dread of weekly Assembly.'

If the fear of official disapproval was not enough, transgressors who lost too many house marks faced detention, during which they had to spend a given period of time reading or writing what they were told to. A worse punishment was being 'gated', which meant not being allowed to go home for the next exeat. It would be misleading to imagine, however, that all girls went about

friends confessed to raiding the biscuit tin in the kitchen. Jackie Ison (Beill) remembered that one of the nuns' favourite punishments for being caught out of bed was having to kneel in the dark in front of the statue of the Sacred Heart for half an hour. She said that the apparent purpose was to shame the culprit into a better, more obedient frame of mind, but that most girls punished that way found it so terrifying that they never repeated the offence.

According to Nicky Hall (Turle), 'There were certain nuns with whom we had to tread carefully or we would be in big trouble. One of my friends coined the lines: "Hush, hush, whisper who dares, Mother **** is coming upstairs".' Mary Kinoulty remembers Mother Rennie's apparently uncanny ability to sense impending trouble. She usually wore flat shoes with rubber soles which enabled her to glide noiselessly down the corridors, leading to her nickname of 'Creeper'. When one girl, unable to find her gym shoes, said 'Damn', Mother Giles came up to her and said very gently, 'My dear, you must not use that word. You must say "How very vexatious!".'

By now sixth formers had much more freedom, both in where they could go and in the hours they could keep. They were allowed into the town on Saturday afternoons as long as they said where they were going and what time they would be back. The Sixth Form flats meant that each girl had her own study bedroom and the new St Joseph's block included a whole floor for their needs: a small reading room, a lecture room and several dedicated teaching rooms. They were also expected to carry out duties as prefects, helping to look after and supervise the younger girls.

The 1966–7 magazine listed a wide variety of clubs to keep the girls occupied in their leisure hours: the choir; the Classical Society, with a focus on Greek and Roman architecture that year; a Topical Society whose members took part in an archaeological dig in the grounds, discovering some seventeenth-century pottery in the process; a Film Club; a Record Club (*The Sound of Music*

The Sixth Form flats in use today as a study and recreation area for sixth formers

rather than the Rolling Stones); a 'Links' group to promote active membership of the church. There were outings to the theatre in Farnham and concerts in London supplementing the usual round of school productions and music. Religious faith and practice, of course, were so woven into the fabric of daily life that they seemed almost taken for granted. It is recorded that 'two-thirds of the school would get up at 7am for early Mass, voluntarily, during the week', and that Jesuits were brought in to answer the girls' questions, so that they were encouraged to develop their own understanding of their faith rather than simply accept didactic instruction. Sodalities were still important in promoting the boarders' religious faith. Different coloured ribbons still denoted the different levels: purple for the youngest, then red, followed by green and finally blue for the full members. Only a few reached the final level: 'The blue ribbons were allocated very carefully to very few… Those who actually made it… had many duties and certain daily prayers, including the rosary and meditations on the Gospel.' Most of the boarders were practising Catholics, of course; the shift from a Catholic majority in the school to a minority was still in the future.

The chapel, looking towards the tribune

The beckoning future: opportunity or threat?

1967 saw the school celebrating an important milestone: the 150th anniversary of the founding of the Order. On 20 May the new bishop of Portsmouth, Derek Warlock, celebrated Mass and blessed the new school block, officially declaring it open (although it had been in use for some time). This event was followed by a garden fete which actually had to be held in the school hall because of a sudden heavy downpour. The fete was designed to help cover the costs of the new building, and managed to raise the impressive sum, for that time, of £1,000. And then in November, Community Feast Day was unusually festive, with a surprise in the grounds for the Sisters: a beautiful Japanese maple called Ozakasuki, bought by the girls and

planted in secrecy with the help of the gardener. The Sixth Form had taken over the nuns' duties in the dining room for the occasion, and had formed the tables into a giant 150, while the bust of Abbé Lafosse was decorated with flowers. Mass was celebrated with a new harmonised chant, composed for the occasion by Mr Pask, and the chapel was crowded with nuns and pupils, supplemented by visitors from Yateley Hall and the local community. The day's celebrations concluded with the Lower Sixth play, a production of Christopher Fry's *The Boy with a Cart*.

They had much to be thankful for: the school had weathered two world wars and the years of postwar reconstruction, and continued to grow and thrive. The school roll had increased by 100 over the previous decade, taking it from a two- to a three-form entry. Increasingly, however, as they looked ahead, questions were being asked

Above: The library winter garden

Opposite: The Japanese maple, planted to commemorate the 150th anniversary of the founding of the Order

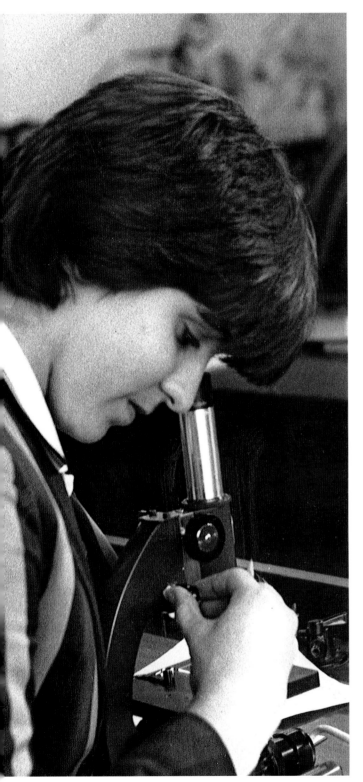

about the form that future would take. Although it was not until 1970 that Mother Alexander openly addressed the issue in a letter to parents and old girls about becoming a comprehensive school within the state system, the possibility of such a transformation was beginning to seem more and more likely.

Less radically, in her Headmistress's Report in 1968, Mother Alexander outlined curriculum changes which had been brought in with the aim of keeping the school abreast of the latest ideas in education. Nuffield Science was being introduced in the lower school, with an emphasis on experimentation and observation. It meant an increased number of animals on the premises for the girls to study: 'Last term it was mice, this term it's locusts and worms – but as long as they stay within the confines of the biology laboratory, I don't mind.' New methods of teaching mathematics were also being experimented with, and the school had offered the less able the chance to sit the new CSE course if they were unable to cope with GCE O level maths. She also reported on the debate about whether to continue with classics teaching, increasingly marginalised since it was no longer an entrance requirement for Oxford and Cambridge. The school decided to carry on, but to shift the emphasis from a strict grammatical approach to a more culturally based course. Classical civilisation was being offered for the first time to enable girls the chance to carry on in English their studies of the ancient world. Language laboratories were becoming fashionable as the focus of language study moved somewhat from writing to speaking. The school was not able to afford a full-scale language laboratory at that time, but the headmistress was able to report on the use of audio recordings and the exciting prospect of exchanges with one of the community-run schools in France.

Addressing the issue, 'Is it the same school?', she spoke of the eternal struggle to 'instil into the girls what I have no doubt they regard as old-fashioned courtesies – such as standing up when an older person approaches them, to say nothing of when a member of the community approaches them; opening doors, standing aside, offering to carry things for others; gentleness in voice and manner. We often feel that we are fighting a losing battle.' Of even greater concern to her was the prevailing mood of 'apathy and resistance to religion and religious practices found now

Left: Science, 1970s

Mother Alexander

As Mother Alexander moved on to become Provincial of the Order in the summer of 1971, Michael Wookey, a parent and long-term governor of the school, paid this tribute to her time at Farnborough Hill:

'The closing of the summer term of 1971 saw the end of Mother Alexander's period as headmistress of Farnborough Hill. Her twelve and a half years in office were years of change, of expansion, of new endeavours. They were strongly marked by her personality. Her connections with Farnborough Hill go back to the two years she spent here in the Sixth Form studying science. She was elected head girl in her Upper Sixth year. From England she went to Trinity College, Dublin, where she obtained a first class honours degree in experimental science. This was followed by research at Oxford and an MA degree. Despite possibilities of joining the family business, she entered the novitiate of Christian Education at Farnborough and was professed at Farnborough Hill in 1954. A month later she was sent to Ireland, where she gained teaching experience under Mother Horan. It was at this time that she obtained a higher diploma in education. In December 1958 she succeeded Mother Hogan as headmistress of Farnborough Hill, being one of the youngest headmistresses ever to be appointed to a public school.

'Her period as headmistress saw many educational changes. In 1961 after several years of negotiation with the local authorities, "scholarship" pupils were accepted from Hampshire and other counties. At first only a few were admitted, but later a third form entry was started to accommodate the larger numbers. In 1958 there were 350 pupils and by

Mother Alexander in 1963, *top*, and, *inset*, as head girl, 1947–8

1971 numbers had grown to 520. Staff had increased in proportion and the Sixth Form, which numbered about fifty at the start of her time in office, had doubled by the end. Mother Alexander introduced sets and parallel forms to replace the previous system of streaming. Tutor groups in the Sixth Form were introduced in 1969.

'Although the building fund appeal made in 1963 was not primarily her responsibility, Mother Alexander played a large part in the design of the extension (St Joseph's block) built between 1963 and 1966.

'An awareness and a concern for the spiritual, educational and social needs of young people characterised Mother Alexander's period in office. The future role of the school is at present uncertain but, whatever the outcome, Farnborough Hill will have benefited from her acute appreciation of the current needs of the time.'

Mother Alexander would usually interview the parents when considering a child for entry to the school before talking to the child herself, and her communications with parents make it clear that she considered their daughters' education a joint responsibility in which she expected them to play their part. Sister Mannion remembers her as fearless in speaking her mind and unworried by criticism of her decisions if she was convinced she was acting for the good of the school.

among young people' and she called upon the parents who listened to her for support. As her remarks made clear, she believed that the true value of Farnborough Hill lay in its religious rather than its academic education.

By 1969, there were definite plans afoot for a sixth form college in Farnborough, planned to open in 1974. The Sixth Form at Farnborough Hill had continued to grow, from twenty-two in 1959 to ninety a decade later, and to counter the 'glamour of the sixth form colleges', further changes were made to enhance the Sixth Form experience. The Upper and Lower Sixth had already been separated and a further division was made into small tutor groups. Teaching groups were divided if there were more than ten pupils and there was even talk of abolishing the uniform requirement; in addition, they had a large common room with coffee brewing facilities, a particularly valued amenity.

All this, of course, might have become irrelevant if the school decided to join the comprehensive revolution

sweeping the country, since the model chosen by Hampshire envisaged the comprehensive schools extending only to age fifteen or sixteen and further study being undertaken in colleges. The school was rapidly heading towards a crossroads. Nearly a third of the school benefited from some form of county grant which helped them to face the burden of constantly rising fees. Now, in the early 1970s, with the decision of Hampshire and Surrey to go comprehensive, no new children would be eligible for grants. The choice was stark: 'If we take one road, we remain an independent school, become progressively more expensive, possibly smaller and therefore less viable, and in doing so there is every indication that we would exclude an increasing number of Catholic children because of ever-rising fees.' On the other hand, taking the other road would mean a profound change in the nature of the school: 'This would mean embarking on comprehensive education as a voluntary-aided school. Like an increasing

number of well-known public schools, this would involve us in co-education in the classroom, although our boarding sector would remain for girls only; we would cooperate with the two Catholic schools in the area (the Salesian College and All Hallows) to provide a Catholic Sixth Form capable of competing with the proposed secular non-denominational sixth form college planned in Farnborough for 1974.'

This dilemma was one faced by independent schools up and down the country in the political climate of that time: would they risk extinction if they could not maintain their roll or should they be absorbed in the new comprehensive system, risking the loss of their individual identities as they faced merger with other local schools? Farnborough Hill at first inclined to the latter choice, and indicated to the Diocesan Education Council their willingness to take part in the comprehensive scheme provided certain conditions could be fulfilled. Were the

scheme to go ahead, the intake of the school would change gradually from the bottom up, with the school not fully comprehensive until 1980.

However, once All Hallows had been accepted as a comprehensive school, the diocese was less interested in having another, particularly one with such an expensive building to maintain. In addition, the uncertainty was harming recruitment and unsettling the staff. For all these reasons, the decision was made to reject the comprehensive option, and the school recruited its first professional lay bursar, Major Dawes, to help with the process of maintaining full independence in the modern era. An additional effect of the debate about the future was the development of the pastoral system which saw, among other changes, the introduction of 'year mistresses' in the lower part of the school, with one year mistress following a year group through for the first three years. This system continues to the present day.

Upper Sixth girls in 2007 enjoying the company of Salesian College boys

The 1970s: a new decade; some familiar problems

In 1971 Sister Dawson, a niece of Mother Mary Dawson Murray, a much-loved member of the Order, took over as headmistress of Farnborough Hill. Her avowed aim was to promote the happiness and unity of the institution at a time of considerable uncertainty about the future. One of her first acts was to overhaul the house system with its division between boarders and day girls. In her first address to parents, Sister Dawson set out her vision for the school: 'I should like it, first of all, to continue to be a happy school… It is this happiness which provides the essential atmosphere wherein a school can achieve the purpose for which it exists, the education and fulfilment of the whole person. It is a corporate achievement in which parents, pupils, staff and Head are inescapably involved. This is an aspect, perhaps the most important, of another quality of the school I should like to see emphasised – its unity… Originally, Farnborough Hill was a boarding school; then day girls were admitted but they were separate from boarders. There were houses for boarders and houses for day girls. There were good administrative reasons why this

should be so at the time. But we cannot think in terms of Farnborough Hill boarding school or Farnborough Hill day school: we are quite simply Farnborough Hill and this is why boarders and day girls are now integrated in the newly named houses of the English martyrs.'

This reorganisation of the houses was plainly not universally welcomed. The final house reports for the former houses began on a tone of regret: 'St John's House died a much lamented death at the end of the Easter term'; 'St James's House ceased to exist after the Easter term. It was sad to think that the old traditions of the houses had gone'; 'Although doomed, as they say, to die, St Catherine's was successful in many directions during its last two terms'. Only St Augustine's turned in its final report without a lament for the house.

Even two years later, the house reports spoke of the upset to house spirit caused by the changes. Becket House's, for example, began: 'The house system has suffered a number of traumatic changes over the last two and a half years, resulting eventually in five houses of 100 girls each from both the boarding and day sectors of the school. Initially these houses were to be subdivided into junior and senior sections, each having their own house committees and holding separate meetings, but this scheme has dissolved into nothingness, never really having got off the ground.' Campion's report was even more negative in tone: 'Two years ago there was, what might be politely termed, a house reshuffle in which the names of the houses were changed and everybody was moved around and generally muddled up. An embarrassing period followed in which house mistresses and house captains alike had difficulty in remembering the new names, but helpful hints in the form of colours were provided: "I'm in… er… blue?"' One problem was that the boarders had more scope for losing house marks, being under constant scrutiny; this remained a source of tension for some years to come.

Another innovation with long-lasting consequences was the 'crash course' in computer programming given to the fifth and sixth formers by a Mr Bolt, 'all the way from Exeter accompanied by an Olivetti Programma 101 computer, an adding machine and a hand desk calculator'. Under instruction, the girls 'went on to write more advanced programs containing simple and conditional jumps'. The visit was organised by the mathematics department who

Sister Dawson

could see the day when their slide rules would be superseded. It is worth noting that the first Apple computer was still five years in the future. By modern standards the Programma was heavy (35.5 kilos) and difficult to use, but by the standards of the time it was revolutionary in being small enough to sit on a desk top and possible for a layman – or girl – to use. It also had the glamour of the space programme on it: NASA had used several in the calculations needed to put men on the moon.

Sister Dawson's speech at the Parents' Weekend in 1975 revealed the same struggle to uphold the principles of Christian education in the face of an increasingly secular society which had so exercised Mother Alexander. The key, as she saw it, lay in being able to 'translate effectively the truth of the religious lesson into the religious, academic, social and administrative structure of daily school life', based not on blind obedience but 'a relationship of love between the individual and God'. She went on to note that the public attitude to religion had become 'less hostile' than it had been a decade earlier, but that girls were still

Opposite: Outside the lower gallery today

Below: The new science labs in 1966

Vera Curran and the Curran Memorial Prize

Generations of girls have won the Curran Memorial Prize for 'Courtesy and School Spirit' but not all remember the teacher whom it commemorates. Vera Curran taught a variety of subjects – history, geography, social studies – from 1959 until her sudden death in the spring of 1971. She had been an Olympic swimmer in her youth, and during the Second World War, while a prisoner of the Japanese in Malaya, she had swum out to tell the arriving allied forces of the plight of her fellow prisoners. At Farnborough Hill she supervised swimming and study hall, organised a film club and was one of the first house mistresses when the house system was developed. Her sudden death during the Spring half term holiday came as a great shock to the school community, and the prize which bears her name was instituted in her memory.

being influenced by 'the materialistic attitudes of our society. "Having" seems more important than "being" or "giving". Consequently, learning to be, to share and to live together is not easy. It involves basic good manners, respect for oneself, respect for each other and for those in authority, courtesy: all of which are essential qualities… Clubs, societies, school events and games fixtures are all opportunities which teach us to work with others, to accept our limitations and to appreciate both our own gifts and those of others.' Coming as it did in a decade notable for civil strife, from the miners' strikes and the three-day week to the terrorism of the Troubles in Northern Ireland, which had seen bombs in Aldershot and Guildford, this call for cooperation and tolerance must have struck a chord with many of her listeners.

Yet, if this all sounds unduly serious, it is plain from both written records and the many reminiscences of old girls that teenagers have always loved having fun. The 1975–6 magazine includes several articles by girls taking an irreverent look at school life – as well as a piece by Clare Rozak remembering the entire Fifth Year 'fainting' during the headmistress's speech in Assembly as an April Fool joke in 1974. She adds that the joke was not well received. If all this suggests a considerable change from the days of sitting in ordered rows and writing notes to dictation, the list of subjects passed at O and A level make it clear that Farnborough Hill was still a highly academic school. At O level, English language and English literature, history, mathematics, religious studies, either French or German and one or more sciences were taken by nearly everyone, while art, food and nutrition, geography, Latin, music, Greek literature in translation, needlework and Spanish were also available. English literature, economics, French and history were the most popular A level choices, but a number did physics, biology, chemistry or mathematics and other traditional subjects such as art and geography.

A series of spoof letters to problem pages reprinted in the magazine gives some indication of the breadth of reading undertaken by the older girls. Then, as now, Shakespeare was on the curriculum (*Othello* and *The Taming of the Shrew*), as were Jane Austen's *Northanger Abbey* and Emily Bronte's *Wuthering Heights*. *Anna Karenina* is a little more unexpected, while light relief is provided with letters from Peter Rabbit's mother and Eeyore, whose complaint in

verse is answered with a tart 'I see quite plainly that you have a persecution complex. It also seems that you have paranoid tendencies', revealing that popular psychology had also formed part of the staple reading.

Claire Harman's jokey 'multi-choice thank-u-letter' (1976–7) hints at the pressures the examination candidates

Claire Harman's 'multi-choice thank-u-letter', 1976

Contents of this letter copyright
The Multi-Choice Thank-U-Letter Co. (Limited)

18 Woodside Road,
Weybourne,
Farnham.
16th August, 1976.

Dear . . . .

I was (delighted (astonished (disappointed (upset (beaten to death by my deranged mother   when my results

arrived, announcing that I had (easily (actually (almost (somehow (only   passed / failed the exam. I'm sure that you will be too.

I am convinced that the marvellous / awful results had little to do

with the amount of work I did / your unceasing efforts and that the credit / blame must go, of course,

to your expert instruction / my own inkonPEta£nse/? or perhaps the examiner was just

(in a good mood   ) .
(dead drunk   when he marked my paper) !
(about to commit suicide   ) . . . . .

Now that the results are known, I am (happy (afraid   to inform you that (forced

I am (preparing to go to university (scraping money together to blackmail the Admissions Tutor with (seriously considering a career in the Foreign Legion

My parents had promised me a gold watch / black eye depending on my results — I'm sure

to get one now. Thank you again for your (help (patience (promise of bail

See you (soon (next January (in the dole queue

. . . .
Claire Harman *(left July '76)*.

felt themselves to be under: 'Now that the results are known, I am happy/afraid/forced to inform you that I am preparing to go to university/scraping money together to blackmail the admissions tutor with/seriously considering a career in the Foreign Legion.' The headmistress, however, was able to tell parents that 'we had a high percentage of success in applications for university places, the vast majority securing places in the university of their first choice. In addition, two girls were offered places in Oxford and three in Cambridge… Other girls find fulfillment and happiness in varying careers: nursing, physiotherapy, journalism to mention but a few.' It is worth remembering that in the mid-1970s a far smaller proportion of students in the country as a whole went on to higher education, and that many practical subjects were not taught at degree level.

A hint of the social turmoil of the times comes in an account by Melody Burke of life during a prolonged power cut, with cold classrooms, cold food and a father unwilling to use his car because of petrol shortages. During what has become known as the 'winter of discontent', the coldest for sixteen years, petrol distribution became an industrial weapon and successive groups of workers – dustmen, car workers, grave diggers, health service ancillary workers – went on strike until the Labour government of James Callagahan conceded defeat on its attempt to cap wage rises below 5%.

At Farnborough Hill, too, normal life was becoming increasingly problematic. Since its foundation in 1889 it had been a boarding school, with day girls forming a minority, especially at the beginning. As the 1970s wore on, however, the number of boarders dropped off as fewer parents wanted to send their daughters away from home. Children of diplomats and military personnel had also been a staple of the boarding school, and in this period of

economic stringency there were fewer overseas postings to make boarding for their children necessary. In addition, fewer nuns were coming forward to replace those who were no longer able to look after the boarders. Running a boarding school at Farnborough Hill meant having the energy to run up and down the stairs all day; instead, more of the community needed to be looked after themselves, rather than looking after the children. As the 1970s came to a close, it seemed clear that the school would have to change.

Facing the prospect that boarders were becoming 'an endangered species', the 1980 magazine included a series of reflections on boarding life contributed by members of the Lower Sixth. Joanna Freeman, for example, remembered 'Fifth year: seventeen of us were lodged in a large partitioned room. During frequent breaks from the monotony of O level work, entertainments were carried

on from flower pot racing with waste paper bins to the usual talcum powder fights and the ritual cleaning up of the lecture theatre after the bath had been allowed to overflow.' Maria Kwong, from Hong Kong, observed, 'I think it is fun being a boarder, but on the other hand we are kept under strict rules. I was quite exasperated at first for we were not allowed to our bedrooms until a certain time; we had a fixed time for hair washing; we had to go shopping in our uniforms; we were not allowed to eat on the streets or else we would be reported; we were only allowed to watch television at weekends… there were so many rules to keep.' Another mentioned 'hard beds, unappetising food, cold rooms, having to rise with the sun at 7.30 in the morning'. Perhaps it should come as no surprise that boarding was losing its appeal. However, these same girls were well aware of the positive side of boarding: 'Boarding, I think, has made us all far more

As a day girl, I used to travel to school on a private coach which took us up the hill and dropped us in front of the school. One morning there was a loud cracking noise and Barry, our coach driver, cursed rather loudly! He had been sweating trying to turn the bus into the drive without hitting Sister Rose's car, which was parked next to the lodge. Unfortunately, her precious vehicle had been hit by our coach. Later that morning I had an RE class with Sister Rose and I was curious to find out how she would react. We were confronted by a tearful and even whiter than ever Sister Rose and ordered to 'Pray for my car, girls, pray for my car'. Needless to say it was very hard for us all to keep a straight face.

Madeleine Howard

independent of our families, but at the same time teaches us to appreciate our parents and brothers and sisters more as we see them less frequently. We all like to feel we belong, and when you are a boarder you can get this feeling. At school you are treated as an individual, not as Mrs X's daughter.' Positive or negative, it was increasingly difficult to continue, and this pressure would grow more acute in the next decade.

I remember my last day at Farnborough Hill in December 1983. I had stayed on to do the seventh term Oxbridge exams, so there were few of us left and little fanfare about our going. It was late on a December afternoon and the lower gallery was dim and quiet, with a light burning by the statue of the Sacred Heart outside the library. As I walked towards the mirrored doors, looking at my eighteen-year-old self, I remembered first seeing my scrubbed and over-awed eleven-year-old reflection when brought to meet Sister Dawson and to see the school. Sitting on an Oak Parlour chair my feet had not touched the ground. That day I left, I felt that I was leaving a house which had become home and the community in which I had grown up. It is difficult to distil why I had been so happy at Farnborough Hill: I had had my share of boredom and tellings-off and detested all games; but a few things and people stand out.

The arrival of Elizabeth McDonald to teach English in 1978 marked the beginning of a friendship which ended only with her death in 2007. Acerbic, elegant and rigorous, unconstrained by any National Curriculum, her lessons ranged freely from medieval history through eighteenth-century gardening to theatrical design, Anglo-Saxon, sailing and theology, leaving us somehow with good results in English and a bit of a crush on her son (whom we had never met) at Ampleforth. Although never one to tolerate laziness or teenage attitude ('This class is arrogant, conceited and boring! Where is your intellectual curiosity?'), she had a dry wit, was always perceptive but never cruel and her classes resounded with laughter. Outside the classroom, her kindness went well beyond duty: in the Sixth Form she was always interested in our outfits; a dance would allow a whole lesson's discussion on the choice of shoes; and she was full of wisdom, which we ignored at the time, about how to deal with young men ('Put yourselves on pedestals, girls; make yourselves a pair of concrete feet.' 'In a mixed college you will fall in love with a young man in your first term, who will dump you in the second and you'll have to meet his other girlfriends.') and royalty ('Curtseying to royalty is optional. If one were to meet TS Eliot, however, it would be necessary.'). Heartbreak would be dealt with with a hug and clean handkerchief and a tough exam with instructions to go home and have a brandy. I'm sure she is missed by many.

She was not the only remarkable character. Madame, in her seventies and having defied Hitler and Stalin in turn, terrified me (and, according to my mother, my father); but sitting with my son to do his prep, her voice came back to me: 'Latin is not just for the exam, it is for life', and I was grateful. Less terrifying was dear Sister Gerety, completely round in her old-fashioned black habit who would, when we were little, button us up and pull our hats down to our scarves before letting us out in the cold. There was also Mr Disken who taught me history: one of only a few men, American and intellectually provocative while Catholic to the core, valuable grit in the oyster.

It was all so much fun; and for a school which might on the surface have seemed strict, it was rarely rigid. I loved 'Talent Night', when the scope allowed for satire was remarkable, with nuns frequently lending their veils for the purpose of utterly irreverent comic impersonations. I loved Mrs Nicholls' art trips to Italy. Given money for ice cream and a warning to be back for supper, we were left to our own devices to see the art or not as we wished: generally we went to see everything, adding in a few adventures of our own. I loved the scope within that building, with its cellars and turrets, and the grounds with their woods and rhododendrons (like rose hedges round Sleeping Beauty's castle) to find space to be with one's friends and, from time to time, to hide from gymnastics class. It's a school which leaves a mark, different on each of us I suspect; but always a mark.

Helen Griffiths

The statue of the Sacred Heart outside the library

High winds and new challenges

As the 1980s opened, the most urgent question facing the community was what to do about boarding; and in the end, the decision was reluctantly taken: to cease offering boarding from September 1981, with current boarders able to stay on for a maximum of two years to finish their O levels or A levels. Hazel Martin, then as now working in the school office, remembers worried parents contacting the school and the scramble to find alternative accommodation for the remaining girls.

With the departure of the boarders the character of the school inevitably changed. Some of the Sisters moved or returned to Ireland to help at the Order's two schools in Dublin and County Wicklow. Others like Sister Mannion stayed on to supervise the domestic staff and run the housekeeping side of the school; she and the other remaining working members of the community continued to live in the school until 1994, when the Farnborough Hill Trust was formed.

For many of the Sisters the departure of the resident girls came as a devastating blow. Sister Hawkins, speaking many years after the event, said, 'It was like death to me when the children went. I missed them terribly. I had no children to put to bed and no lights were on.' Others, like Sister Mannion, took a more pragmatic view: 'Children should live with their parents' was the way she put it, though she has many happy memories of the 'lovely girls' whom she helped to look after. By contrast Sister McDonnell, though very fond of her charges, found the new freedom at the end of the day quite liberating. In her early years as a boarding mistress she had been expected to sleep in the same room as the girls she looked after. Now she was allowed to have a little privacy: 'it was just a little room, but it was lovely being able to close the door.'

Sister Mannion and Sister McDonnell at a garden fete, 1980s

had stayed. Built? All the accommodation given over to dormitories… is now utilised for educational ends.' Jackie Ison (Beill), a former boarder and later PE teacher at the school, once startled a class by pointing to a corner of what is now IT2 and saying 'This is where my bed was in the first year'. The Sixth Form flats were given as study rooms to members of the Sixth Form and the RE and art department, IT and technology gradually colonised what had been boarding rooms, while the piles of un-needed bed frames moved first to the attics and later were discarded altogether.

One of the more gradual but important changes brought about by the ending of boarding was the shift in the religious character of the school. Almost all of the boarders as well as many of the day girls had been Roman Catholics, but this now changed. The school retains its essential Catholic ethos, but also welcomes girls from a wide range of faiths and traditions. Mrs Berry remembers that in the 1970s all non-Catholics were excluded from Mass and instead sent upstairs to do their homework if there was a service during school hours. During the 1990s, by contrast, the chaplain, Miss Downes, was faced with a delegation of Protestants who asked to be excused from the by-now compulsory Mass. As a compromise, she agreed to put on a special service for them to be led by an Anglican priest. In the event he was unable to come, but the service went ahead anyway and 'they prayed their little socks off'.

A further change in the composition of the school came about when the decision was made to join the

New uses for former dormitories in the 1980s

Above left: The cubicle dormitories of the new 1960s block became the home economics rooms

Above: The study bedrooms of the 1930s had become common rooms by the 1960s and then the computer room by the 1980s

Left: The top floor dormitories became the art studio

Mary Brister, in her supplement to Mother Mostyn's *The Story of a House*, and a member of staff at the time, noted: 'The departure of the boarders inevitably changed the character of the school. Gone was the influx of girls from abroad and those whose parents were serving overseas, and hence the diversity of cultural experience which they brought. Although the house would hum until late in the evening with many extracurricular activities, thereafter it would be largely dark. On the other hand, one now wonders how on earth we would have coped if the boarders

newly created Assisted Places scheme, which provided scholarships for girls who could not otherwise afford the fees. This broadened the social mix of the school and also provided some welcome stability in the finances, which had been stretched somewhat since the removal of the 11+ system more than a decade before. The increasing popularity of the school meant that every five years an extra form was added so that some year groups were much larger than others. Although this provided more girls with the opportunity to attend the school, some felt that the 'X' form, as it was known, was never fully integrated into the school community. Part of the problem lay with the name itself: so different from the regular A, Alpha and Omega. Some believed it stood for 'extra'; to avoid this sense of difference, when the school moved permanently to a four-form entry some two decades later, the new form was named B.

The 1980s saw the establishment of a new senior society, 'Le Cercle Procope', which was founded by Mary Brister, head of English, and Connie Anscombe, head of maths. Their aim was to promote and stimulate intellectual and cultural interests among selected sixth formers, and was based, as the initial article explains, on the Café Procope in the Rue de l'Ancienne Comédie in seventeenth-century Paris: 'It soon became a popular meeting place for the wits, poets and intellectuals of the capital. Among those who met there were Voltaire, Diderot and other Encyclopédistes' … continuing through the French Revolution with 'Marat, Danton, Robespierre, Talleyrand and Bonaparte'. While the Farnborough Hill clientele was never expected to start

In 1986 Emma and I were in a school production where we were supposed to go off the stage, dance around the audience and elbow a few parents with the greeting 'Alright guv'nor' and invite/drag parents onto the stage to join in the Lambeth Walk. Unfortunately only one dad succumbed to the persuasion of one girl (not even his own daughter) and ended up on stage on his own with the Year 2s. Poor guy!

My favourite thing about Farnborough Hill is the amount of laughing I did – and chatting! That was what my report always said, anyway. I was in most of the school productions and got the giggles on stage in all of them. In *The Boyfriend* my friend George and I were part of the Year 2 chorus that started off the second half. We had to dress in fancy dress and George and I chose to be bank robbers with eye masks.

The only problem was that every time we blinked the masks moved up our faces so that we were unable to see after a while, and of course every time we looked at one another we started to laugh. Coming to Farnborough Hill was at first like going to Malory Towers or St Clare's. To join a class where we were known as a 'form' was like acting out Enid Blyton.
Anna Payne (Bowyer)

Hurricane hits England

The autumn of 1987 had been unusually mild and wet and most of the trees were still in full leaf in October. In the early hours of the 16th, Sister Rennie was woken by the skylight above her bed in her small room at the top of the old house rattling violently. Anxious only for a good night's sleep, she attached a heavy suitcase full of books to the latch of the skylight by means of a stout belt. This did the trick and she peacefully returned to bed. The next morning, still unaware of what had happened, she was surprised to field a series of phone calls from girls and staff asking if the school was open that day. What she only discovered later was that hurricane-force winds had ripped through southern England during the night, killing twenty-two people in England and France, uprooting fifteen million trees, downing power lines and toppling thousands of chimneys. Sleeping beneath a glass skylight at the top of one of the tallest buildings in the area would not seem to have been the safest spot that night, but this she only discovered afterwards.

The 1987 hurricane caused extensive and quite expensive damage to the roof of the old house, which was no sooner repaired (with the aid of a government grant) when three years later in January 1990 another bout of stormy weather struck. Jacqueline Thomas, then deputy head and later headmistress, described the scene vividly: 'As deputy head, I would often pop into the staffroom towards the end of lunchtime as it was a good opportunity to chat to colleagues. When the bell went for afternoon registration, I became conscious of the noise from the adjoining quad and went out to chivvy the girls along. I shouted and they all scurried off, leaving the area deserted. I had only just stepped back into the staffroom when there was a mighty rumbling, like thunder getting louder and louder, followed by a tremendous crash. A number of us rushed out to see what had happened. The quad was filled with dust and debris, the roof was in splinters and suspended above it was the bell tower, which had fallen from the turret.

'Obviously we couldn't let the girls back into the quad but it was a cold, windy day and they needed their coats before going home. In the end Mrs Berry and I lined the girls up, one class at a time, and taking each girl's key went ourselves to retrieve essential belongings from lockers. My overriding memory of that operation is the smell of apples. Many of the lockers were leaning at crazy angles and as we opened them we were showered with overripe apples which the girls had scrumped from the nuns' orchard and stored on the top shelves. It was just as well that Mrs Berry and I were unaware at that point of just what a risk we were taking. Subsequent investigation revealed that the bell tower was resting very precariously on the remaining struts of the quad roof.

'I remember the day the imperial eagle was finally raised back into position on the top of the turret. A giant crane was positioned outside the kitchen door. The most complex part of the operation coincided with break time so I went outside, ostensibly to keep the girls out of harm's way but actually to get a closer view myself. As the eagle was slowly raised it began swinging rather alarmingly, and one of the workmen shouted "Watch out for the chicken"!'

Views of the bell tower, *left*, the clock tower, *far right*, and the wrought-iron ornamentation on the top of the house, *right*

Below and right: The tower provided a source of artistic inspiration for one student in 1989. The school magazine that year showed both a photograph of the artist at work and the result of her labours. The view from her vantage point a year later would have been very different

revolutions or found philosophical movements, it was hoped that the combination of intellectual discussion and sherry might prove stimulating to the more intellectually inclined of the Sixth Form. With a mixture of outside speakers and home-grown ones, the group listened to papers and discussed topics such as 'Crime and punishment', 'Technology and society' and 'Radioactivity and nuclear power'.

They met after school in the Oak Parlour (now the headmistress's office) and the society proved very popular – with those who were invited. Membership was by invitation only, based on O level (later GCSE) results. This could throw up some anomalies: former English teacher Rae Robbins remembers that when she arrived at the school the deputy head girl was a member but the head girl was not. Since membership – and the stimulation provided by the discussions – proved useful on UCAS applications, there was understandably some resentment among those excluded. Mrs Brister retired in the early 1990s and Jo Russell, her successor, agreed to take over the society only on the strict understanding that it would be open to all. It was, but times had moved on and it faded away a few years later, though something of its spirit of broadening horizons with outside speakers lives on through the Think Tank talks of the twenty-first century.

Mrs Brister had other ways of raising standards. Members of her department vividly recall the importance given to letter writing and correct forms of address in their schemes of work. Girls were taught how to write to bishops, members of parliament, different ranks of the aristocracy and company directors. As Mrs Robbins explained later, 'They were being prepared to be the wives of great men.' An alternative interpretation, of course, is that Mrs Brister wanted them to be able to hold their own in any social situation. It is not recorded how many girls actually went on to use these skills.

Sister Dawson, who had been a very young headmistress, had left in 1983 to become the youngest Superior-General since the congregation's foundation. Her place was taken by Sister Sylvia Cousins, who had taught in the school eleven years previously. She came at a time of great upheaval in education, with the former examination system of GCE O levels and CSEs being replaced with GCSEs. One of her innovations was to introduce more specialist teaching rooms arranged by subject. Up to that point, younger girls had mainly stayed in their own form rooms with teachers travelling to them. Now, with the need for ever more sophisticated facilities to accommodate a more active and less text-based curriculum, it became increasingly important for subjects to have their own spaces for storage and display.

As she reported in 1987: 'The examination system is undergoing major, far-reaching changes, the role of schools in society has become the focus of attention and teachers are coping with increasing pressures in the classroom. Many parents are fearful that standards will not be sustained, that Christian values will be diminished and that the school curriculum may not meet their children's real needs.' If all this sounds a little melodramatic, it is worth remembering that it was not just GCSEs which were being introduced. A whole National Curriculum was being

imposed from above, complete with (eventually) SATS tests at regular intervals throughout the child's time at school. Farnborough Hill, as an independent school, was not obliged to follow the National Curriculum, but the changes to examinations affected everyone.

For their part, the girls adapted well to the changes, as Sister Cousins was able to report. GCSE, with its emphasis on group work and coursework, suited many girls much better than the 'everything depends on one exam' ethos of O level. However, a worry was how well the new examinations would prepare students for the unchanged A levels. This was of particular concern in science where it was now possible for girls to follow a 'combined science' course; mathematics, too, required more of a step up than previously. However, Sister McCormack, who had replaced Sister Cousins as headmistress in 1988, was able to report the following year that the Sixth Form 'guinea pigs' seemed to be 'coping well with A level studies', and this positive trend continued over the coming years.

With new examinations came new subjects – or at least new ways of teaching old ones. Music technology appeared on the curriculum and the school purchased two video players and some electronic keyboards. Technology in general was on the ascendant, and former subjects such as domestic science and needlework were replaced by food, textiles, wood (later resistant materials), information technology and graphics. Even computers were starting to make an appearance. By 1989, 'all girls from the Fourth Form upwards [were offered] short courses in typing and word-processing – and a secretarial course to those sixth formers who are taking not three but two A levels'.

Sister Elizabeth was in post during the important centenary year of 1989 when many celebrations took place, not least a visit from the Cardinal Archbishop Basil Hume. His arrival at Farnborough Station to celebrate Mass in the chapel unfortunately coincided with a bomb scare, and Sister Rennie remembered the consternation of the welcoming party up at the school as the minutes ticked away. Eventually he arrived with only five minutes to spare, but despite this stressful beginning the Mass was a wonderful occasion, remembered by all who were there. The cardinal knew the school from his days at Ampleforth, which was attended by many of the boarders' brothers. In addition, he knew many of the Farnborough Hill sixth

Sister Elizabeth McCormack

Sister McCormack came to England in 1967 on a one-way ticket from Dublin. She studied first in Southampton and then later at Exeter; even during her time as headmistress she continued her academic studies, reading for a Dip Psych from Maynooth. At Farnborough Hill she taught history and was later head of religious education, served as a head of year in the lower school and head of Howard House, then became Superior of the community and later the school chaplain before becoming headmistress in 1988.

Jacqueline Thomas, her deputy, has written warmly of their relationship: 'Looking back, I can say that I had the greatest fun during my first ten years at the school when I worked alongside Sister Elizabeth.' In addition to reinstating prize giving as an important event in the school calendar, under her guidance the school joined the Independent Schools Careers Organisation (ISCO), and helped to encourage girls to explore the world of work through Young Enterprise and Neighbourhood Engineers. Modern languages expanded under her leadership and Anne Griffiths was appointed to lead an expansion in technology and science.

Sister McCormack remembers her period in office as a time of profound change in education: 'the introduction of the National Curriculum, league tables, Personal, Social and Health Education (PSHE) and Records of Achievement (ROAs) to name but a few'. There were other challenges too: 'Like many other religious congregations engaged in education, vocations to our Order had diminished and I knew there were no Sisters to follow me in leadership. Consequently I believed one of my responsibilities was to prepare the school for lay management.'

As headmistress, Sister McCormack very much missed the daily contact with girls which was, for her, the most fulfilling part of a teacher's job. However, she knew all of the girls by name, and devoted herself to helping each one to develop her individual gifts and talents, while at the same time nurturing the spiritual life of the school. She instituted the Birthday Book 'to ensure that every girl had her name read at Assembly. Prior to this it was only the high achievers and girls who were members of the sports teams who had their names called out. I wanted every girl in the school to feel recognised, valued and respected for who she was as a student of the school as well as for achievement.'

Sister Elizabeth displaying a watercolour presented to her by a pupil on the occasion of her retirement, 1996

One innovation which Miss Thomas remembers less fondly was the start of a Parents' Newsletter, designed to improve communication with parents, since responsibility for its production fell to her as deputy head. The first edition was just one typed sheet with a hand-drawn letterhead, but it became the precursor of today's professionally printed, full-colour booklet. Open Afternoons also began, to give parents the opportunity to visit the school a number of times and to get to know it before their formal interview with the headmistress.

As part of a growing professionalism in the world of education, Sister McCormack successfully led the school through a quality and management audit by the GSA, resulting in two excellent inspection reports from GSA and HMI. In 1996, she decided to move on to fresh challenges, and stepped down as headmistress. However, after a sabbatical, Sister McCormack joined the Board of Governors of the school, eventually becoming its chairman. She is now a trustee.

formers who regularly travelled with Sister McCormack to his monthly meetings with young people in London.

Other commemorative events were a gala reunion for old girls, complete with a display of old photographs and reminiscences which were on show from May to December. Mary Brister's account gave some sense of the festive party atmosphere that year: 'On Parents' Day, exactly 100 years

after the first three Sisters had arrived from France, Joan Walters' pageant presented the history of the Order and of the school in Farnborough from the beginning. On the Feast of the Sacred Heart, 400 people wined, dined and danced the night away in a house transformed for the evening for the Friends' splendid Centenary Ball. On 17 September the hall swarmed with 700 happy old girls. Anne Robinson,

Governors, trustees and bursars

Orchard Rise

Once the Farnborough Hill Trust was set up, the school became more dependent on members of the lay community. Of particular importance were the governors and trustees, who in turn relied on the bursar.

Since 1994 the chairs of governors and trustees have been Michael Wookey (1994–9), Peter Wilson (1999–2011) and Michael Maher, who was chair of governors from 2003 to 2011 and since then has been chair of trustees. He was succeeded as chair of governors first by Sister Elizabeth McCormack (2011–12) and then by the current chair Jonathan Hull, whose daughter attended the school from 1998 to 2005 and was head girl.

Commander Tony Woolston has been the longest serving bursar and has successfully steered the Farnborough Hill ship since 2001. In that time most of the new buildings have been commissioned, and it is down to his excellent financial management that these developments (the Mother Alexander Sports Hall, St Anne's Art and Design Centre, St Joseph's, the Theatre on the Hill and St Cecilia's Music Suite) have all been brought in on budget and largely to time. Previous bursars who also played a crucial role in keeping Farnborough Hill solvent through challenging times include Dr Gerrard Berry (until 1994) and Lt Col John Henwood (1995–2001).

dedicated, experienced lay teachers as more and more members of the Order retired. And therein lay the problem. Although a remnant remained on site, helping to run the school as before, they were too few in number to carry on the burden unaided. Something needed to be done.

In 1994 the Farnborough Hill Trust was formed, which gave the school a legally separate identity from that of the Order. The community still owned the land and the buildings but offered them to the trust at a modest rent on a very long lease. As Miss Thomas described it later, 'The transfer to lay management was carefully planned and managed by the Religious of Christian Education in a way which could put other religious orders to shame. As a teaching Order, their commitment to the education of girls remains paramount and they ensured that the handover went as smoothly as possible with Farnborough Hill's future secured. In particular, the wholesale transfer of financial assets enabled the school to embark on a rolling programme of capital development.'

With this shift in responsibility, the remaining resident Sisters moved down the hill, either to Lafosse or to Orchard Rise, the small detached house formerly occupied by the school secretary. One practical consequence of this move for the staff was that it suddenly became much easier to move around the building. The remaining Sisters had been based in or near what later became the caretaker's flat over the kitchen, and that whole part of the school was consequently out of bounds for teachers.

who turned up, had mentioned the reunion in her radio programme, so helping to ensure a large attendance.'

The final decade of the twentieth century inevitably saw fresh challenges. In many ways the school was thriving. It continued to recruit well, aided by the Assisted Places scheme, and the examination results held up well under the new arrangements. The staff room was filled with

---

When I first went to Farnborough Hill the community still lived in the building, in the part which is now the caretaker's flat. That gave the school a very special feel as it was also home to the Sisters. Every morning they stood at the pupil entrances – the quad door, the lobby door and what is still known as the day girls' entrance – to greet each girl as she arrived. I remember one parent telling me that she still wasn't sure whether she'd chosen the right school for her daughter when they arrived on the first day of

term, but all her fears were banished when Sister Hawkins greeted the nervous newcomer with open arms and the words, 'Here comes another of my little ones'.

The same care also extended to the staff. Working late at night in my upstairs office, I would sometimes be surprised by Sister Rennie, who would arrive in her dressing gown to bring me a very welcome mug of hot chocolate. On one occasion, however, I had walked over to the green gallery late at night to

set up for an A level examination in the morning. It was pitch black up there but as I was carrying the large 'silence' notices I didn't trouble to turn on the lights. I knew just where I was going and had no fear of the Empress Eugenie's ghost. I was unprepared, however, for the silent but sudden apparition of Sister Rennie. I dropped the notices in shock, exclaiming, 'Oh, my God!' 'No,' admonished Sister Rennie, 'it's just me!'

Jacqueline Thomas, then deputy head

Sweet dreams

In 1995 Maggie Catterall answered an advertisement for a manager to take over the running of the school tuck shop. Until that time the shop had been open for only twenty minutes a day during morning break and stocked a limited range of goods. With the formation of the Farnborough Hill Trust, however, the bursar, Colonel Henwood, saw the opportunity to expand it to meet the increased demand from pupils and teachers. The job description specified that it should sell 'phone cards and lunch tickets' but added that the manager should 'be innovative and entrepreneurial'. Maggie, as she soon became known, responded and the glory days of the school tuck shop began.

Sweets had always been the core business of the tuck shop, certainly as Sister Mannion remembers it, but now Maggie provided a much larger range – all available for a penny each. Healthier options such as fresh fruit were also always provided as an alternative, but never proved as popular. But with the new millennium came an increased focus on children's diets and worries about the amount of sugars and fats that they consumed, so the headmistress, Miss Thomas, asked Maggie to modify what she sold. A more limited range of inexpensive sweets appeared (inflation had put the price up to 5p) but these were supplemented by muesli bars, sandwiches and chocolate bars.

The original advertisement, which mentioned selling 'phone cards and lunch tickets' was very much a reflection of the era. The phone cards were necessary if girls wished to make phone calls from the single public call box available to them; mobile phones have long since taken over, but dinner tickets are still dispensed from the tuck shop, even if they have moved from being on paper to credit on the fingerprint access system in the dining hall.

With the ever friendly and approachable Sister McDonnell, Maggie greets every girl and helps to keep a discreet eye on the vulnerable or unhappy. The tuck shop has always been a social place where friends from different years can meet up on neutral ground. Many old girls keep in touch with Maggie and are eager to share their fond memories.

Alexandra Fontaine who started her financial career with a rival business carried out clandestinely says:

'In the first and second years I was an "occasional boarder" which meant I befriended the boarders while predominently a day girl. This was the best of both worlds as there were different rules when it came to the tuck shop. Boarders were only allowed to spend 10p a day in the tuck shop while day girls had no restriction. I was popular because, when I was sleeping at school, I would arrive in the dorms with huge supplies which I shared with everyone when lights were out. I'd discovered a gap in the market. As a day girl I could buy sweets and crisps on behalf of boarders, unbeknown to Sister McDonnell. Every morning break I would be found queuing in the tuck shop and would then come out with armfuls of goodies and distribute them to my school friends. They paid upfront and placed their orders, which I meticulously wrote down. No doubt the paper had been ripped out of an RE exercise book. Secret distribution took place in the far corner of the junior quad or in the piano cells. What was my payment for losing hours of break? I didn't demand cash. My commission was in sweets and crisps.'

Maggie Catterall with Sister McDonnell in the tuck shop

The ghosts of Farnborough Hill

One Halloween, late at night, a little girl crept from her bed in her dormitory. She moved cautiously along the green gallery, descended the main staircase, her feet padding softly over the wooden treads, and made her way silently along to where the tapestry of Our Lady Queen of Heaven hung on the wall. She had heard the stories of the Empress Eugenie returning once a year to put another stitch into the work, which she had left unfinished at her death. Were the tales true? She was determined to find out. After waiting for some time in vain, the lure of a warm bed became too much and she turned back. As she did so, a distant figure in white came gliding towards her and she screamed. What she had seen, as the nuns who came rushing to her aid explained, was her own reflection in the mirrored doors of the library. The legend was a potent one. Other girls, over the years, had attempted to help the story along by leaving out needle and thread or even inserting stitches of their own, so that the community was eventually forced to protect the tapestry under glass.

Above: The Empress's tapestry which hangs in the lower gallery

Right: The green gallery

Below right: The red corridor

The neo-Gothic architecture of the building, the creaking floors and the winding passages are made for the telling of tall tales – and indeed there is a remarkable range of unexplained phenomena, experienced not by hysterical teenage girls but by sober members of staff and the community going about their daily work. Moreover, these stories, all independently recounted, centre on particular parts of the building. The main staircase and green gallery, the upper floors around the IT area, the red corridor and the vicinity of the kitchens all seem to have unexplained activity, while the newer parts of the school seem free of ghostly apparitions.

One of the most striking tales is recounted by Hazel Martin, now the school secretary. One winter afternoon she was doing some filing in the cabinets under the main staircase when she felt a touch on her shoulder. She turned and saw Sister Mullen looking at her, dressed in full habit with veil as she had in life, but with grey robes rather than black. As soon as she recognised her, the figure vanished. Mrs Martin remembered being admonished by Sister Mullen in the 1980s for moving too quickly through the lower gallery to answer the front door. Her apparition also appeared briefly in the lower servery area of the refectory, when one of the cooks was startled to see a small nun looking fiercely at her before vanishing. Her description of the figure, whom she saw clearly, closely matched Sister McDonnell's memory of Sister Mullen. Helen Woodason also reports seeing a dark figure in the lower servery area out of the corner of her eye, and Adam Cartledge, husband of Kay Cartledge-Clark, reported feeling very uncomfortable when helping out there after the

bazaar, as though he were 'an intruder'.

Another focus of paranormal activity seems to be the red corridor. The rooms were used as nursing facilities for wounded soldiers during the First World War, and the noises and movement of objects seem to date back to that time. Sister Mannion reported that some residents of the corridor had heard a sound like tablets being dropped on the floor. The green gallery at the head of the main staircase and the upper floors of the original house also seem to be

haunted. Sister McDonnell remembers seeing a white figure standing at the foot of her bed once while she had a room in this part of the old building.

In her 1993 prize giving speech, Sister McCormack reflected movingly on the character of the school, using the old story of the Empress's unfinished tapestry as a starting point. 'There is a tradition among the girls that the ghost of the Empress returns to put more stitches in it. The younger and more gullible girls study it closely and fancy that they can see new stitches. I feel that the school is like that tapestry made up, in all its richness, by so many different stitches. Each girl represents one stitch in the tapestry, each one unique and each contributing to the whole. Every year our first years put new stitches in the tapestry of Farnborough Hill as they make their special contribution to the life of the school. During the years I have been here, I have never seen any changes in the Empress's tapestry, but the school changes all the time as generations of girls pass through. To our leavers, I say go out and put your stitch in the tapestry of life, use your gifts and talents to enrich society and make the world a better place.'

Most of the reported hauntings involve noises only or objects being moved by invisible hands, but occasionally other former residents of the house have appeared. Helena Rix (formerly Miss Donnelly) recalls making her way out of the house via the service door next to the kitchens, when the shadowy figure of a man reached out and opened the door for her, then vanished as she turned to thank him. Mrs Woodason also recalls an unusual incident at that same spot. She had arrived for work very early in the morning and left her bicycle at the foot of the ramp leading up to the kitchen, just inside the door. Suddenly the bell over the service door began to ring, and as she made her way down to answer it her bicycle bell also began to ring, despite there being no one in the passage. Heavy footsteps have also been heard in that corridor and along the passage which once connected the kitchen with the servants' hall.

Jon Taylor, the school chef, is regularly visited in his flat in the front lodge by two small children, a boy and a girl from the Victorian era. Within the school itself, he recalls an afternoon when he was working on his computer in the office near the kitchen. Suddenly and without warning, the cards hanging from the shelf above began to swing wildly before one was whisked off and flung to the floor, as though by a disapproving hand. Some, like Rob Wallis, the caretaker who lives inside the building, stoutly maintain that all the moving doors and other phenomena can be put down to the natural changes of air pressure and draughts which occur in old buildings. That may well be the case in some instances. However, who was it who tapped on Mrs Martin's shoulder or opened the door for Mrs Rix?

The Empress's tapestry on display
in the chapel, 1954

Prize giving

When Miss Thomas joined the school, she was surprised to discover that there was no annual prize giving ceremony. These had been held in the past, but not since 1939. In the intervening years, the equivalent event had been a speech by the headmistress followed by the school drama production at the parents' weekends. These annual events had ceased when the boarders left in 1981, so Miss Thomas had a free hand to devise a new ceremony from scratch. Prize giving was moved from the summer term to early November so that the fifth and sixth formers could receive their examination certificates as well as any prizes they had been awarded. Her aim was to 'recognise and reward pupil progress, participation and achievement', while the headmistress, Sister McCormack, 'was equally insistent that prize giving mark achievement in music, sport and drama, contribution to the community, school spirit and service as well as academic excellence'. All examination students would be invited, along with their parents, so that everyone would have a chance to attend at least one. Since there were a great many prizewinners from other years too, the chapel became so full that, in 2012, the juniors were given their own ceremony one afternoon in the final week of the summer term. The guest of honour at the first reinstated prize giving was Dame Shelagh Roberts, 'authoress, ex-Euro MP and feminist', as she was described by a member of the Lower Sixth. Since then the school has welcomed a widely varying range of inspirational speakers, including Professor Susan Greenfield and the school's own Olympic bronze medallist, Alex Danson. An old girl of the 1930s, Mary Rose Murphy, felt moved to reflect on the final prize giving service held in the school, in July 1939, when she was 'the last girl to get a major prize at the last Hillside prize giving'.

Old girls present the prizes at prize giving: *top*, in 2010, Dr Anne-Marie Drummond, Fellow of Lincoln College Oxford; and *above*, in 2008, Dame Helen Ghosh, now Director General of the National Trust

Sister McCormack continued as headmistress until 1996, but then left for a sabbatical before moving on to a career in social work. Her place was taken for a year by the school's first lay headmistress, Rita McGeogh, and then by Jacqueline Thomas who was eventually succeeded by the current headmistress, Sarah Buckle. Miss McGeogh's period in charge coincided with the ending by the newly elected Labour government of the Assisted Places Scheme. Under the scheme, nearly a third of girls had had their fees paid for them. Now, although the existing scholarships would be honoured, no new girls would be financed, so other ways of filling the roll would have to be found.

Matters were in so parlous a state that when Miss Thomas became headmistress in 1997, she was warned by the governors that she ought to draw up contingency plans for redundancies. Instead of doing so, however, she decided that her aim would be to rescue the school by recruiting more students, and to that end persuaded the governors to allow her to hire a marketing director. 'I remember recommending to the governors that we appoint a development director and being asked what he would do

Girls from Farnborough Hill protesting at the G8 summit held in Coventry in 2000 as part of a delegation of Sisters and sixth formers from Farnborough Hill. They helped to form a chain of prayer around the city to bring attention to the effects of third world debt

all day! Apart from countering the assumption that the development director would inevitably be male, I was able to assure the board that it would be a full time job, as the two holders of the post, Jan Evans and Clare Duffin, will testify.' Teaching staff, initially sceptical at the prospect of the added expense of a new member of the senior management team, were won over as the numbers of new girls entering the school began to grow again. Recruitment became so successful that in 2000 more students were accepted than could be accommodated in the usual three forms. The decision was made to add a permanent fourth form and the school has had a four-form entry ever since.

Miss Thomas
with girls, 2007

One of Mrs Evans' innovations which very quickly bore fruit was the introduction of 'Busy Bees Day', which gave potential recruits a chance to experience for themselves what life on the Hill was like. With specially printed T-shirts in colour-coded groups, the excited nine- and ten-year-olds tried their hands at specially designed tasks like solving a mystery with the aid of chemistry clues and orienteering around the grounds with the geography department.

As the year 2000 approached, the school decided to mark this milestone in the Christian calendar with a range of special events. In place of the usual day-long retreats, a special team came to the school with activities for an entire week. Later in the summer, the RE department arranged the transport of the entire school to Wintershall to see the famous pageant of 'The Life of Christ'. That summer an old girl, Mary Rose Murphy, donated a 'millennium yew', said to have been grown from a cutting of a thousand-year-old tree, to be planted in the school grounds. The girl selected to plant it was Harriet Whittingham, the youngest girl in the school, who remembers the event well: 'As Miss Thomas read out my name, I'm sure she was expecting the other Harriet to stand up as she was small and petite while I was the tallest girl in the year. I had to stand in front of the school, collect the tree after it had been blessed and carry it down the hill with the whole school following behind. A small plot had been prepared and I placed it in the ground and we then filled all of the soil around it. I remember being incredibly nervous in case I dropped it.' The tree continues to grow, albeit slowly, fourteen years later.

I had a woolly sheep hanging on my doorknob with 'Come In' embroidered on the front of his jumper and 'Do Not Disturb' on the back. One morning I found that my woolly sheep was gone and a ransom note, composed of letters cut from the newspaper, had been pushed under my door. I waited until the end of Monday Assembly and then I announced that I'd a serious matter to raise with the school. As I explained what had happened and the girls gauged my mood, an unnatural hush fell on the hall. No one wanted to catch my eye or draw attention to herself by so much as a cough for fear of being accused of the offence which so angered me.

Only gradually did it dawn on them that my anger was feigned and I wasn't serious about suspending all privileges until the culprit stepped forward. Gradually a ripple of laughter spread through the hall, starting in the tribune. Some days later I was in the staff room at break when I was told that my woolly sheep had been seen dangling above the lobby door. That was no surprise as the Upper Sixth flats are located two storeys above.

I walked outside nonchalantly and, when I arrived at the lobby door, reached to retrieve my sheep. He danced upwards, just beyond my grasp. I jumped and there was a howl of excitement from girls standing around the tree stump. This brought more spectators running up the hill. Clearly there was no dignified way out so I kept on jumping, to the delight of the crowd, until the end of break when my woolly sheep was released from his line and fell into my arms.

Jacqueline Thomas, headmistress 1997–2007

Technology: typewriters to laptops

Miss Thomas reflected on the revolution in communications which took place during her tenure at the school: 'My career at Farnborough Hill very much spans the coming of the computer age. I can hardly believe that tools I take for granted today didn't exist when I first came to the school. The office staff were still using typewriters although I inherited a state-of-the art Amstrad which allowed me to do a little more sophisticated word processing. I also had the use of a BBC computer which could be used to upload the timetable I'd created on a wall-mounted board. I still remember the rolls of computer paper which churned though the machine printing out staff, class and room timetables in indecipherable code.

'As in most schools, computing for pupils was introduced thanks to the enthusiasm of a self-taught member of staff. Lynda Cadby, a maths teacher, presided over a room full of BBC computers, which provided the first taste of a new approach to education. As these machines became redundant with a speed we had never foreseen, the difficult decision had to be taken on the purchase of the next generation of class computers.

Mrs Cadby decided to go down the Mac route on the grounds that the operating system was more intuitive and child friendly. However, by the time we were ready to replace the Apple machines it had become clear that PCs ruled the world, or at least the world of education, and a change of direction was called for.

'In fact, the speed of change in this area was one of the foremost challenges throughout my time at Farnborough Hill. As the hardware consumed large sums of money, it was essential to make capital purchases wisely and with an eye towards future developments. By the time I retired we were just in the process of installing interactive whiteboards in all classrooms, shifting the focus from dedicated computer rooms.' And so the process goes on, with notebooks in the school library and ever more sophisticated smart phones owned by the students and teachers in place of one large, cumbersome and inefficient school-owned mobile phone which had to be checked out by teachers who were leading school trips in the early to mid 1990s.

Far left and left: The St Anne's painting and textile studios

Below: The Mother Alexander Sports Hall

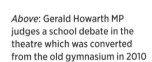

Above: Gerald Howarth MP judges a school debate in the theatre which was converted from the old gymnasium in 2010

Below: The fitness suite in the sports hall

If September 1997 had been a crisis point in the history of the school, with an alarming dip in recruitment, the position changed completely in a remarkably short period of time. Three years later, in September 2000, the new first year had expanded to four forms due to increasing demand for places. By 2005, with the extra revenue additional students brought, the school was at last in a position to begin building again. The first project was a new sports hall, named in honour of Mother Alexander and opened by Bishop Crispian Hollis in September 2005. The building included a sports arena big enough to hold several classes at once, together with modern changing rooms, a classroom for examination teaching, a fitness room and an office for the PE staff. These new facilities allowed the conversion of the gym in 2010 to a theatre with the addition of tiered seating, curtains, a new high-tech lighting and sound system and a striking pink-lit glass screen at the entrance. This theatre, now called 'The Theatre on the Hill', supplemented the smaller 'Princess Studio' and provided a versatile new performance space.

Lafosse House and the Religious of Christian Education

The Sisters of Christian Education were the backbone of Farnborough Hill for the first century of its existence and beyond, providing the headmistresses, the teaching staff, the support staff and those who looked after the boarders. The school was their home, from their first arrival and often to the end of their lives; the nuns' cemetery in the grounds was for many their final resting place. By the 1970s, the rooms above the refectory with windows giving on to the chapel had been designed so that sick or elderly nuns could lie in bed and participate in the Mass being said below. The older members of the community who were not bedridden then used as a base the area above the kitchen known as St John's, now the caretaker's flat, leaving the former community room free to become a music room. What is now the prayer room was created as a small private chapel for the Sisters who could no longer get up and down the stairs easily. However, it became apparent that a more

Opposite: Lafosse House, 2013

Right: Residents of Lafosse House, 2001. Left to right: Sister Wright, Sister Rennie, Sister McDonnell, Sister Elsa, Sister Eileen Clarke, Sister May Shannon, Sister Joan Gerety

permanent arrangement was needed for the nuns who were no longer able to take part in the daily life of the school, and so in the early 1970s the Order commissioned a new, purpose-built retirement home on the site of the now defunct school farm near the walled kitchen garden.

Lafosse House, named after the founder of the Order, opened its doors to the first residents in 1974. It included eighteen comfortable bedrooms on two floors with wide corridors and grab rails and a beautiful modern chapel panelled in natural wood in which they could hear Mass daily. The pattern of religious life, with its daily prayers for the school, maintained a vital link with the institution to which they had dedicated their lives. Sister Rennie was put in charge of the Lafosse House community and Sister Dawson, later Sister Josephine, of the school community who were to remain in residence to look after the boarders.

Christmas 2004 at Lafosse House

Left: Sister Eileen Clarke

Below: Sister Bridget Scully

Bottom: Sister May Shannon

A photograph of the early Lafosse House residents shows all of them in the traditional black habit with veil, despite it being nearly a decade after the dress reforms left them free to wear more modern habits if they wished (see pages 144–5).

Their position within the grounds of Farnborough Hill gave the residents a view, albeit a distant one, of their old home, and regular contact with the school. Those who were able continued to attend Mass when it was celebrated in the chapel, and Community Feast Day, 21 November, was celebrated as it always had been. Even after the end of boarding in the early 1980s, this tradition continued, until the ordeal of coming up the hill to a noisy pantomime became too much for some of the Sisters. Eventually, the entertainment was modified to become a much quieter and more varied musical and dramatic programme given still by members of the Lower Sixth, as an accompaniment to a tea party in Lafosse House itself. This gave successive groups of sixth formers an important chance to get to know some of the Sisters who had worked so hard for generations of their predecessors. Sister Elsa, for example, kept one group enthralled with her account of sprinkling holy water in front of the window in order to protect her charges in the dormitory against intruders who she feared might climb up the magnolia trees that grew by the wall.

Titles and habits

In the early years of the school, the title of Mother was used to denote the 'choir nuns', whose roles in the community consisted of teaching or administration and who often had degrees or other qualifications. Those who carried out the domestic work of the community were known as 'Sister'. Eventually, following the reforms of Vatican II in the 1960s, it was decided to remove this distinction. The 1966–7 magazine records, 'All the nuns are now addressed as "Sister" except the Superior of each house and the Novice Mistress, who are called "Mother", and the General and Provincial Superiors, who have the title of "Reverend Mother".' Claire Scargill (Nicholson) recalls this period of transition: 'During my time at the school the nuns changed from being all Mother to being Mother for the teaching nuns and Sister for the others, which we all rebelled against strongly. Then they became all Sister apart from Reverend Mother and then reverted to all Mother. Quite a lot to get used to over seven years!' At much the same time, the nuns were given the option of abandoning their traditional dress and so the distinction in occupation which had been visible in their habits also disappeared.

An early photograph, taken in the grounds of Hillside, shows Mother Caroline Murray, one of the founder nuns of the school, together with her sister, Madame de Villalonga, and another nun. Their long cloaks and stiff white 'bonnets' worn without veils look decidedly French in character and reflect the Order's origins in Normandy, where the habit was apparently modelled on the costume traditionally worn by widows. This French influence is also evident in the names given to the various items of dress: the bonnet and sur tete, both worn under the veil, and a black cape called a pelerin. A slightly later photograph, taken in the woods behind the school, shows the evolution of the head-dress to include a smaller

Above: Detail from an early photograph taken in the woods at Hillside

Below left: Sister Rennie on the right with fellow nursing Sisters from other orders in their different habits, early 1950s

bonnet, tied under the chin, together with the pelerin and veil. A slightly modified version of this habit remained the norm until the 1960s.

Sister Grant, a postulant in the 1950s, remembers going shopping locally to buy a black skirt and blouse. When she became a novice she exchanged this simple outfit for a long black habit with a white veil, which was replaced, after final vows, with a black one worn over the white starched bonnet and sur tete. As a choir nun, her sleeves were larger than those of the lay Sisters. She remembers the bonnet affectionately, for the way it helped her to focus in prayer and to avoid distractions.

Sister McDonnell was one of those who helped maintain the spotless white bonnets in the linen room of the school. They were made of layers of white calico, starched, folded and ironed to make a smooth, stiff frame for the face – as long as it remained dry. As she puts it, 'If you got caught in the rain, you had had it', as you were left peering out from behind a wet curtain of calico. Beetroot and other highly coloured food could also be a problem. The habits were made by the Sisters themselves, and each individual only had two: one to wear and one in the wash. One of the older Sisters used to collect all the habits each summer to soak them in a decoction of ivy leaves in order to restore the black colour.

The bonnets were so time-consuming to make and so restrictive in what they allowed the wearer to see (driving and even bicycle riding were impossible) that they were eventually exchanged for a simpler white wimple and black veil. Further changes followed in the wake of Vatican II, and after some hesitation the nuns abandoned their long black skirts for something more modern and easier to move about in. As early as 1967 the

head-dresses which covered the hair but left the face exposed, making it possible to drive and move about freely. Later, when the Spanish bronze became unobtainable, they moved to green skirts and tops. In recent years, many have started wearing a range of colours and styles including, in Sister Grant's case, very stylish trouser suits. All, however continue to wear the RCE crucifix and ring, and some, such as Sister Wright, continue to wear a head covering as a visible sign of their vocation. Sister Hawkins continues to wear the black skirt and blouse, together with the black veil, and this adherence to past traditions reassures some of the old girls whose memories of the Sisters are indelibly bound up with their distinctive costumes.

NEW HABITS FOR NUNS

Above: Sister Rennie, pictured centre, in the old-style bonnet which framed the face, but did not allow the wearer to look sideways without moving her head. The new, simpler bonnet was easier to maintain and less restrictive

Farnborough News report, 1962

school magazine mentions a visit from two American members of the Order, both wearing what is described as 'the experimental contemporary habit'. A report from the sister school in Clermont in 1982 rather provocatively asks, 'Are our nuns human?' and goes on to describe a recent fashion show in which a novice from Dublin and the Reverend Mother General took part to show off 'the new short length habit and vest. Oh, how audacious they were compared to the voluminous black habits our Sisters wore. The most daring thing of all was the veil. Who could have imagined nuns having hair?' The report concludes, 'What a huge advancement – and the Religious of Christian Education took it with humour and grace – and some of them have very shapely ankles.'

The new habits, designed by a fashion designer from Dublin, consisted of a mid-calf length skirt and jerkin in 'Spanish bronze', a sort of khaki-green fine worsted fabric. The Farnborough Hill nuns had theirs made by Collyers in Aldershot and wore them with cream blouses and simple

Sisters at Farnborough Hill Convent are wearing the modernised habit recently adopted by their order, the Institute of Christian Education. Here, the Reverend Mother discusses plans for the new school year which opens on September 20, with the headmistress, caterer and infirmarian. Members of the Order work in France, Ireland, U.S.A., and North and West Africa as well as in England. The Convent, originally known as Hillside Convent, opened its first school in this country 73 years ago, at Star Hill, Farnborough. In the first decade of this century, the nuns built the large school which was, until recently, the R.A.E. Technical College and is now part of Farnborough Technical College. They also erected the building on the other side of the road. (NA861)

Sister Wright

I was born in Farnborough in 1924. My parents already had a daughter, and my mother, in particular, was rather hoping for a boy. However, the Irish midwife presented me to my mother as 'Paddy, the next best thing'. The name Paddy stuck and I was christened Patricia Rosemary.

Farnborough Hill, way back in 1929, had a junior school attached, so I started in the kindergarten and never had to go to any other school. I wanted to do PE or nursing when I left school, but my doctor said I was not strong enough for either of these careers so I ended up working in a bank. When I was at school I had thought about becoming a nun, but not really seriously. It was only after I left, when I often used to go back and visit the Sisters, that my thoughts deepened and I finally decided in 1945, during the summer, that I wanted to enter the Order. I saw Reverend Mother Roantree and Mother Horan, who were happy and told me to pray about it, and of course that I had to tell my parents. I knew my father wouldn't mind, but I knew also that my mother would probably blow a fuse. It was coming up to my twenty-first birthday and she was planning a big party which I did not want. My mother did her best to dissuade me from entering, and in the end I said I would only have the party if it was a farewell party as I was entering on 6 January – though I didn't eventually manage to enter until 2 February. It was rather an upsetting day: my father was very unhappy because my mother wouldn't say goodbye to me, and for a long while she did not write to me or come and see me.

In the last six months of my novitiate I was sent to France to join the novitiate there. I phoned home the day before I was going to ask my parents to come and see me. My father answered the phone and said he would come and I begged him to ask my mother to come as well. I said many prayers that she would agree, and was actually at the altar of Our Lady in the chapel when one of the Sisters came in to tell me

my parents were here. Much to my surprise, I found my mother walking arm in arm with Reverend Mother Roantree as if they were old friends reunited. Certainly my prayers had been answered.

I was professed in France on 21 November 1948 and I returned to Farnborough Hill on 7 December that year. It was good to be back for Christmas. I was given a dormitory to look after and I helped each day in the junior school. In September 1952 I went to the Royal School of Needlework where I embarked on a three-year course. But by the middle of the summer term it

was thought that London did not agree with my health, so I sadly had to leave the Royal School and went to Ireland where I stayed for thirty-three years, first helping with the opening of the school in Dublin and then, in 1956, with the opening of the boarding school in Co Wicklow. About 1965 I was back in Terenure in charge of the junior school where I stayed for ten years and really enjoyed it. Then I went back to Clermont until August 1986 when I came to Lafosse House, where I have now been for over twenty years – and as you can see I am still going strong.

Sister Rennie

Veronica Rennie came with her sister as a boarder to Farnborough Hill in 1936 from her home in Burgess Hill. Miss Rennie, as she was then, left in July 1944, following secretarial training, intending to get a job in an office.

After three weeks, however, she was phoned by the school asking her to help with their school in Salisbury. Her call-up papers followed her there, but by the time they arrived she was back at Burgess Hill visiting her family. During the interval before the papers followed her to Sussex, she decided to join the Order, a decision she says that she has never regretted.

Sister Rennie had enjoyed English while she was at school, but the Order decided that she should develop her talent for science and should prepare for a science degree at Queen's College in Kensington by taking an accelerated School Certificate in physics and chemistry. This proved to be inadequate preparation, so instead she trained as a nurse in St John's and St Elizabeth's hospital in St John's Wood. She worked there for four years, and remembers an influx of patients from the extensive flooding in East Anglia in 1952, as well as one of the notorious London smogs which was so bad that ambulances could not bring the injured to hospital; even though all the windows were closed, the pollution in the wards was so bad that she could not see the clock on the wall.

In 1953 she returned to Farnborough Hill as the school matron, which kept her very busy. On one occasion, 120 out of 160 boarders were in bed with the flu, and she had to call on other members of staff to help look after them and keep them entertained. Following the establishment of two schools in Ireland, she also spent eleven years at Clermont, the boarding school in County Wicklow, before returning to Farnborough Hill in 1986 to help look after girls and Sisters alike.

At the Mass of Thanksgiving for Lafosse, 2013:

Back row, left to right: Sister McDonnell; Sheila Farmer, chaplain; Sister Mannion; Bishop Richard Moth; Father Tony Sultana; Abbot Cuthbert Brogan; Sister Marie France Everard; Sister Josephine Shannon; Sister Mary Dawson; Sarah Buckle

Front row, left to right: Sister Eileen Grant; Sister Rosemary O'Looney; Sister Marie Therese Coursol; Sister Wright; Sister Elizabeth McCormack

Sister McDonnell

Sister Philomena McDonnell arrived at Farnborough Hill from her home city of Dublin in August 1963. This was her second trip to Hampshire as in 1958, just after her profession, she had been sent to Yateley Hall to look after the boarders – but only for a year as she, a city girl, hated the country isolation. Farnborough Hill, though much bigger and in a more urban setting, was also something of a culture shock at first. The community was well established and at first she admits that she was a little nervous of the older Sisters as she herself was still in her twenties. Despite these challenges, she remembers feeling at home by Christmas and has long been an integral part of the Farnborough Hill community, remembered fondly by generations of past pupils.

Sister McDonnell's main responsibility was looking after the dormitories of the younger girls, who all slept on the top floor or in rooms off the green gallery. During term time she had little privacy, being expected to sleep in the room with the girls with only a moveable screen between them. If they woke in the night, they would come to her bedside and there was always much excited comment about seeing her without her veil on. She would supervise the girls' bedtime, then retreat to the bathroom for ten minutes of quiet reflection before creeping into bed in the dark. She was always up in the morning well before the girls, so would be washed and dressed before waking them. Privacy only came after the end of boarding life, when she was free to have her own room upstairs.

The daily routine described by Sister McDonnell appears not to have changed much from the school's earliest days. The rising bell would sound at 5.20. The community would gather for morning prayers and meditation in the chapel at 6.30. After this would come breakfast preparations: cutting the bread, setting up the dining room and getting out the milk and cornflakes. After this the girls would be called for Mass at 7.20 followed by breakfast for all, including the officiating priest. This was usually one of the Benedictines in the Abbey, who was rewarded with a full cooked breakfast.

When the girls departed for their lessons, the dormitories would be cleaned and tidied before the main work of the day began. This might be running the tuck shop, acting as sacristan, helping to clean the sanctuary (which had to be done on your hands and knees) or working in the linen room, which entailed repairing and ironing the clothing of the girls and the Sisters. Sister McDonnell also looked after the quad, which acted as the day girls' cloakroom and informal recreation area. This gave her a chance to get to know the day girls, with whom she would otherwise have had limited contact. She continues this responsibility to the present day, greeting the girls as they arrive and keeping a discreet eye out for signs of distress or other problems. The Sisters also got to know all the girls at lunch, where they moved round the tables by rota so that they could be sure of meeting them all. Friday was 'dormitory night', when the linen baskets with the week's clean washing were unpacked and distributed.

Sister McDonnell and other younger members of the community continued to live in the school until the formation of the Farnborough Hill Trust in 1994, when she went to live at Lafosse House where she took great pleasure in the company of her new companions: 'It was wonderful living with the older Sisters, taking advantage of their years of experience', she says. They taught her to 'take your time and you will settle', and their company helped to enhance her own prayer life. On the closure of Lafosse House, she moved into Orchard Rise. She was offered the chance to move back to Ireland, but has chosen to remain in Farnborough, her home for fifty years, to continue her ministry in the parish and with the girls.

Sister Teresa Hawkins

Sister Teresa Hawkins arrived as a young nun from Ireland in January 1939 and was in charge of one of the boarding rooms throughout the war. When she arrived from Ireland there were about thirty-five nuns in the community. Postulants and novices slept in the attic room at the top of the tower which she remembers as 'freezing' in the winter, but gave wonderful views over the surrounding countryside. After the war she continued to look after the boarders as well as helping in the kitchens and doing many other housekeeping jobs in the main house. She also taught needlework. 'The only job I never had was sacristan' was how she put it. Generations of girls responded to her motherly kindness and she in turn was devoted to them. Sister Hawkins also worked for a time in the Order's schools in Ireland, but eventually retired to Lafosse House where she continued to keep a motherly eye on the school and the girls who came to visit her. When Lafosse House closed in 2013, she moved to the Holy Cross care home in East Sussex.

By its nature, Lafosse House had quite a high turnover of residents; in 1984 alone, four Sisters died. And as the years went by the inevitable departures were no longer compensated for by new arrivals, though with the formation of the Farnborough Hill Trust former residents of the school like Sister McDonnell moved in to help look after the more elderly members of the community.

Nicky Hall (Turle) remembers the 'bed for the night' which she enjoyed in 2004 and which turned out to entail the exclusive tenure of the west wing, along with 'a large lunch just for me set out in the dining room'. By 2012, it was clear that Lafosse House was no longer viable. After Sister May Shannon elected to return to Ireland, the resident population had dwindled to four: Sister Eileen Grant, Sister McDonnell, Sister Wright and Sister Hawkins. The decision was made to close the building and disperse the remaining occupants. At the time of writing, the fate of the building has yet to be decided.

Sister Hawkins was the first to leave; in June 2013 she moved to a care home in East Sussex, bringing to an end an association with Farnborough Hill which began in 1939. She was too frail to return, but Sister Wright, Sister Grant and Sister McDonnell were guests of honour at a special

Sister Eileen Grant

Sister Eileen Grant was educated at St George's School, Ascot, but came to Farnborough Hill at the age of eighteen along with her identical twin sister in order to do an advanced secretarial course. She then worked with the MoD on radio- and radar-related projects while maintaining a busy social life at dances in Camberley. Her interest in theology, first kindled by encountering the writings of St Thomas Aquinas, developed as she read more widely. Eventually, in 1956, she entered the Order and was sent to the newly opened school in Clermont, Co Wicklow, for her postulancy and novitiate. Then, back in England, she went to Froebel College, part of the Roehampton Teacher Training College, to train for three years before moving to Yateley Hall, where she taught from 1962 to 1982.

Even while maintaining a full teaching load at Yately Hall, Sister Grant was called upon to use her secretarial training to help the headmistress, Mother Alexander. She can remember typing all the correspondence concerning new girls up until the time when they actually arrived at the school, including sending out the results of the Common Entrance examination, and also did all the filing. After the closure of Yateley Hall, Sister Grant was personal assistant to the principal Roman Catholic chaplain of the army for twenty years until 2003. On her retirement and return to Lafosse House, she continued to work part-time for a number of years, helping to administer a Catholic army trust fund and overseeing the archives of the Catholic army chaplaincy. Her Majesty the Queen awarded her the MBE in December 2004. Sister Cara Nagle, Superior General, accompanied her to Buckingham Palace for the investiture on 7 June 2005.

Sister Mannion

Sister Monica Mannion comes from Claremorris, Co Mayo, in the Irish Republic. She joined the Order on 6 October 1962, choosing the Religious of Christian Education because of her desire to work with young people. During the first eight years of her religious life she worked in Clermont and Dublin. At Christmas 1970, she travelled to Farnborough Hill for the first time with a small group of nuns; she remembers feeling the cold keenly after the comparatively mild temperatures of Dublin, to which she returned with relief after Christmas. Partly for that reason she was less than delighted to be informed the following month that she would be posted to Farnborough Hill. Sister Mannion

though she says she still prefers running the stationery office. Moving out of Farnborough Hill itself into the modern and compact Orchard Rise was less difficult than she expected. One delightful novelty was how easy it was to make a cup of tea compared with the corridors and stairs of Farnborough Hill which lay between her room and the kitchens. She still comes up to the school on a daily basis to run supervised prep in the library and carry out many other tasks as well.

remembers the one-way ticket on which she travelled to her new home with Mother Alexander. It indicated to her that she was leaving Ireland for a long time.

She worked as a dormitory mistress, first supervising a dormitory and later the sixth formers in their flats. Life had moved on for the dormitory mistress; Sister Mannion found that she was not expected to sleep in the same room with the girls, but had her own separate space. She remembers that the boarders often had pets to take care of; indeed, a small pet cemetery remains in the grounds, which houses the remains of numerous mice, guinea pigs and gerbils. There was one funny incident when a group of boarders kidnapped Sister Cahill's dog, Bunny, and sent her a ransom note, demanding chocolate to secure his release. Sister Cahill duly paid up – but with just one bar to be shared among the kidnappers.

Sister Mannion ran the tuck shop and also the stationery office, which she still runs. After the boarders left she was kept busy supervising the domestic staff and running the housekeeping side of the school. She also took on the job of sacristan in the chapel, and it was then that she began arranging flowers, one of the tasks for which she has become famous –

service in the school chapel in October 2013 to mark the closure of Lafosse House. However, the Order has not withdrawn completely from the school grounds. Orchard Rise remains as a home for Sister Mannion, Sister Rennie, Sister Josephine Shannon and Sister McDonnell.

Above and right:
Sister Mannion and
Sister Josephine

Sister Josephine Shannon

I came to Farnborough Hill in September 1973, when it was still a boarding school. I had an aunt, Susan Shannon, and a sister, May Shannon, in the Order. Sister May moved from Lafosse House to Ireland in 2012. I joined the teaching staff, and worked both in the RE and maths departments until 1994. I was also house mistress of Campion House until the early 1980s, when I took over the provincial bursar's work from Sister Margaret Bickford.

The Friends of Farnborough Hill were set up to organise fundraising activities. I remember the wonderful Flower Festival weekend, opened by the Papal Nuncio, when the library, gallery, dining rooms and chapel were transformed. The Friends launched a programme to set up a Bursary Fund with the aim of raising £100,000 but with the commitment and generosity of the parents, friends and old girls, they managed to raise over £200,000. As time went on, their fundraising was used to improve the facilities. As Sister in charge of the community, I was on the committee and my biggest contribution was being responsible for the annual raffle. We would be disappointed if we did not make £1,000 or more clear profit, and more as time went on. I used to give a treat to the group who sold most tickets – perhaps a minibus trip to the theatre in Guildford or ice-skating in Richmond.

We were all very excited about Pope John Paul II's first ever pastoral visit to England in 1982. There was a special event for all religious and priests which took place in the grounds of Digby Stuart College, Roehampton. We were all able to attend it and the weather was lovely so we had Mass in the open air. Shortly after this Sister Mary Dawson was elected the new Superior General, the first ever Irish/English person to hold the post. The centenary of the school, 1989, was a year when all activities took on a more festive hue. I was delighted to mount an exhibition in the lower gallery and grand salon. There was a special old girls' reunion, and Cardinal Hume came in November for a special Mass, followed by refreshments.

Above: The whole school make cards for the Sisters on Community Feast Day

Right: Sister Mannion's talent for flower arranging is especially evident on feast days

4

The new century:
growth and development

Towards the future

In the summer of 2007 Miss Thomas decided to retire and
Mrs Buckle was appointed as headmistress. The school was
on a much sounder footing financially than when Miss
Thomas had taken over ten years before, but there were still
many issues that Mrs Buckle had to face in her first year.
Sixth Form numbers needed to be increased and the school's
facilities needed to be updated; and it was an additional
great sadness that she and the school community had to
cope that year with the deaths of two long-standing teachers,
Farhat Soakell and Jackie Ison (Beill), both of whom had
managed to keep up their connections with their students
for a long time while bravely battling illness.

Previous page:
F'Hill Radio
broadcasting from
what was originally
the Empress's
bathroom

Left: 2012 Diamond
Jubilee celebrations

Above: The bell
under the gabling of
the clock tower

Right: The
Millennium Mass

Science lesson in
the new chemistry
lab, 2010

The summer term of 2008 brought a GSA team of inspectors, who wrote a glowing report about the school and the education it provided. Despite the usual stresses of an inspection week, the inspectors' reports made gratifying reading: 'A dedicated and talented staff combines with enthusiastic and well-motivated students to create a community that pulsates with activity and endeavour… The staff teach enthusiastically, imaginatively and very effectively. The school provides outstandingly good pastoral care. Pupils of all ages develop outstanding levels of spiritual, moral, social and cultural awareness.' The lead inspector said that his overriding impression was that the girls were 'very happy and that they had great fun while learning'. That sentiment is echoed by present and past students who enjoy activities such as sledging down the hill during snowy weather and dressing up for charity days, as well as a wealth of music, drama and other activities.

In her first prize giving address to the school in November 2007, Mrs Buckle reflected on the school's academic successes, which had placed it in the top 10% at A level and the top 5% for GCSE results when 'value added' was taken into account. Using her background in

psychology, she was able to tell her audience, 'It is clear that the girls thrive here. There are many reasons for this but two of the most important are that it is a girls' school and it is a Catholic school.' However, despite the positive and helpful 2008 inspection report, an immediate challenge facing the new head was the major worry of the governors at the time that the Sixth Form was in decline. They were anxious that Farnborough Hill should not become a school catering only for pupils aged eleven to sixteen as this would change its character completely. Mrs Buckle's experience as head of a very large and successful Sixth Form at a previous school made her especially qualified to deal with this issue, and she promptly set about rebuilding the Sixth Form through a wide variety of initiatives. It was not long before numbers doubled, and growth continued until the Sixth Form became the viable and stimulating entity it is today. And of course this increase in numbers brought in substantial additional funds which allowed the school to embark on an extensive new building programme.

Together with the new sports hall, the initiatives now being undertaken were the first major developments at the school since the new wing built by Mother Alexander in the 1960s. The old swimming pool changing rooms were replaced by more modern and much more attractive

Head of RE, Helena
Rix (Donnelly), on
the left, and head of
art, Rosemary Byrne
(Pocock), second
from right, at the Art
Exhibition in
St Joseph's 2013

facilities in 2007, which allowed the resistant materials area to expand into the vacated space. Across the courtyard at St Anne's, in what had been the tractor shed, large glass doors were installed to make new painting and textile studios. Ceramics was thus able to expand into space previously occupied by the painters, and new computers next door allowed graphics to be taught on site as well. Four years after he had blessed the sports hall, Bishop Hollis was once more called upon to perform the official opening ceremony, in November 2009. The chemistry laboratory and prep room were completely refurbished in 2009. The following year, the GL1 and biology laboratories, together with the biology prep room, were also refurbished, providing much brighter facilities than those remembered by generations of girls.

In the mid 1990s, some of the attic rooms at the top of the old house had been converted into Sixth Form teaching

Above: Outside the art studios

Above right: Painting by A level student 2013

Below: The Sixth Form common room

rooms. A decade later, in 2009, the Sixth Form was presented with an impressive suite of rooms in which to relax. The Empress's bedroom became a common room, complete with television, leather sofas, dining table and (for a while at least) a goldfish bowl. Next door they had a large kitchenette for producing endless cups of coffee and hot chocolate. In 2011, the Empress's bathroom became a radio station, 'F'hill Radio', making the Sixth Form presenters local celebrities as the younger girls tuned in before school and at lunchtime. Yadin Chowdhury, a Year 7 in 2013, wrote enthusiastically about it: 'Every Monday, Wednesday and Friday, we get to listen to one of the best things about Farnborough Hill: F'Hill Radio. It's so great listening to tunes and chilling in the form room.'

Modern IT systems gradually worked their way around the old building. In 2007 almost all classrooms had interactive whiteboards installed, used with varying degrees of enthusiasm by members of staff: a far cry from the era, just ten years before, when teachers had had to sign up in advance to use one of the two video recorders in order to show films or television programmes. F'Hill Radio uses the IT network to broadcast to every classroom. In 2010 all the school's data was uploaded onto a new management information system, 'iSAMS', and thereafter reports and registration took place electronically.

There were also two major new build projects. The first, the St Joseph's Courtyard development, was completed in November 2011, to provide a large multi-purpose building that includes a dance studio, a new geography classroom, a Sixth Form science laboratory and a new science office. It also includes a celebration of the whole school in the form a beautiful mosaic, consisting of over 600 ceramic tiles, each one designed and made by a member of the school

Above: Some of the tiles that make up the whole school mosaic in St Joseph's

Left: Laptops in use today

Saint Joseph's Courtyard

Blessed by Bishop Richard Moth
February 2012

+ To the glory of God +

Below: St Joseph's
Courtyard and its fountain

community: governors, headmistress, pupils, teachers, office staff, support staff and Sisters. The remaining outdoor courtyard space, meanwhile, was repaved and planted with an attractive range of flowers and small shrubs, with a spherical fountain in the centre.

St Cecilia's, the
new music suite

Technology was very much in mind when the new music suite, St Cecilia's, was being designed. Completed early in 2014, it comprises a music technology suite, teaching rooms and a large heptagonal practice and performance space, jutting out into the Holly Bush Lawn from the side of the chapel. It provides the music department with its first purpose-built facility, offering up-to-the-minute recording and mixing facilities in a striking modern building. It was blessed and officially opened by the new Bishop of Portsmouth, Philip Egan, in April 2014.

The school library, housed in one of the most elegant rooms of the old house, received a face-lift in the summer of 2013. Jo Wood and Mary Wilson, the two librarians, toiled for weeks to box up and remove every book so that it could be cleaned and redecorated. The Grade I listing of the building meant that any renovations were subject to strict planning regulations, but the faded dark wallpaper was replaced with paler blue/green silk. Phase two of the renovations, scheduled for the summer of 2014, involved installing more IT facilities and better seating.

Alongside these major changes, the administrative staff have been provided with improved accommodation, and the heating has been enhanced; no more can staff and pupils complain of the prevailing cold. And in the grounds, a floodlit astroturf hockey pitch is in the planning stages.

And what of the girls during this time of renewal and improvement? 2009 saw the challenging introduction of a new timetable, with fewer, longer lessons – a twenty-five period week replacing the former fifty-three period week. Around this time the school abandoned the old form numbering system; Form I is now Year 7 and so on up the school, though the Upper and Lower Sixth Forms retain their titles. And, perhaps of more immediate note to the girls themselves, the uniform has undergone a transformation, with some of the most hated items (often cited by potential pupils as a reason not to choose Farnborough Hill) replaced with much more congenial modern styles (see pages 162–3).

A Mass in
the chapel

Left: The school at Hillside, late 19th century

Below: A Sixth Form group wearing the tunics and girdles of the 1930s

Uniforms

Say 'Farnborough Hill' to most people who know the school and an image of a green striped blazer pops into their heads. Farnborough Hill has been synonymous with its 'deckchairs' and green skirts for so long that most of the present students imagine that this has always been the school uniform. However, an early photograph of staff and students taken in the woods behind Hillside shows a very different story. Rows of girls sit or stand demurely, hands neatly folded, all wearing long full skirts, high buttoned boots and high-collared pleated blouses with leg-of-mutton sleeves. Sodality ribbons around the necks of the older girls provide the only ornaments.

Farnborough Hill in the 1930s was principally a home for the boarders and Sisters, while the lessons shared with day girls took place down the road at Hillside. To reflect this distinction the two sets of girls wore uniforms in different colour schemes: blue and green for boarders, brown and orange for day girls. Sister Rennie, as a boarder, wore a navy-blue school tunic held in with a green sash or 'girdle' and a striped tie in the school colours of blue and green. The striped blazer was also introduced around that time, and so the 'deckchair' era began. Day girls wore

brown, box-pleated tunics with brown and orange girdles, peach blouses and brown and orange striped ties. They also had blazers, plain brown with a monogram on the front pocket, or straight brown overcoats with big buttons in the winter. With this went brown gloves and a brown beret which had to be worn straight, ie not at a fashionably jaunty angle. Summer saw both day girls and boarders changing into panama hats and printed cotton dresses, which varied over the years from green gingham checks to plain via floral prints which clashed with the striped blazers of the boarders. So important was this colour distinction that the separate school houses were known as 'blues' or 'browns'.

This visible distinction between day girls and boarders persisted even after the move from Hillside at the outbreak of the Second World War. It was eventually abandoned after the war under pressure of continued clothes rationing, when elements of the two were incorporated into a single green and brown uniform for all. The magazine for 1947 refers, for the first time, to boarders and day girls rather than blues and browns. The new uniform consisted of an A-line, knee-length green skirt, green jumper with brown and light green stripes on the v-neck, a white blouse, a green and brown tie and a blazer with brown and dark and light green

Left: Ann Berry's mother, who was also a pupil at Farnborough, studying at home in the 1930s, wearing the day girls' uniform

Left: Day girls 1924 – Edith and Elsie Jones, aged 16 and 14

Above: On the right, Jennifer Lake (Barnes) – Elsie's daughter – in 1957, aged 17

stripes. Regulation underwear included thick white panties worn under thick green gym knickers, and 'American tan' tights. Teresa Luscombe-Male remembers that they had to carry a comb and handkerchief at all times, and that the gym knickers had a pocket in them for this purpose. Quite how girls were expected to maintain their modesty while searching for a handkerchief isn't entirely clear. But then as now, girls tried to shorten their skirts by rolling them up at the waist.

If some items of the uniform have been added, others have disappeared over the years. The striped tie was abandoned, as were the white gloves for formal wear, though Bernie Fife-Schaw remembers wearing them into the 1970s. Last to go was the beret, which presented such a tempting target for the Salesian boys to snatch. Boarders were required to own a white dress for wear on formal occasions, including Speech Days and the Corpus Christi procession. Sister Rennie remembers some of the older girls rebelling as the century went on, resorting to appearing in their tennis whites as an alternative.

By 2006, demand for change from girls and parents revealed that the most hated items were the brown lace-up shoes and the fawn tights. A comprehensive redesign was therefore undertaken by Miss Thomas, Mrs Griffiths and Mrs Duffin, who looked at a wide choice of green and black striped fabrics before deciding that the addition of a narrow purple stripe made the whole look 'less funereal'. Shoes were now to be black, with black tights or white socks, and to go with the new-look blazer the green skirt was remodeled and the brown and light green stripes on the jumper neckline replaced by two narrow green stripes. Lengthy arguments about shirts not being properly tucked in were avoided by introducing a simple shirt with a green piped collar which was designed to be worn outside the skirt. Out too went the 'womble' duffle coats which girls complained were heavy without being warm. Instead a lighter, shower-proof school coat with a hood appeared.

Inevitably, the changes did not please everyone. Losing the brown in the uniform meant severing the last link with the original uniforms of the day girls of Hillside. Some older sisters, or even mothers, had hoped to

pass on their blazers to younger members of the family and could not now do so. The old blazers occasionally turn up in strange places, for example recently on a Japanese fashion website! However, most of the reaction has been favourable, even if girls continue to try to circumvent the uniform regulations.

Uniform, *left*, prior to the 2007 redesign; and *below*, as it is today. Girls have lollies on the Feast of the Sacred Heart

Refurbished chemistry
laboratory

In the midst of all these changes the life of the school went on, with the yearly round of classes and examinations, assemblies and Masses. Though the school welcomed an ever-wider range of religious affiliations, the essentially Catholic ethos remained unchanged with all girls studying religious education for GCSE and religious studies playing a part in the Sixth Form curriculum as well. How it was taught, however, changed and developed. A photograph taken in the newly open 'Our Lady's Wing' shows a class in the early 1950s being taken for religious instruction by a nun. Over the years the subject changed to religious knowledge and finally religious education, philosophy and ethics, which, as Ralph Wellington, a member of the RE department, explains, 'doesn't imply a fixed body of information to be learnt but a study of what religion is, what it teaches and how it affects people's lives'.

Pope Benedict visited the United Kingdom in 2010, and Mrs Buckle and Hannah Martin were given the opportunity to represent the school at the 'Big Assembly' held at St Mary's University College in Twickenham, while the rest of the school watched via video link in the hall. Sister Mannion was also at St Mary's, representing the community. Hannah, reporting back afterwards, said that another young member of the Portsmouth diocese's delegation seemed more impressed by the visiting celebrities than by seeing the

The Odyssey

During April 2010, the classics department led a trip to Greece to tour the ancient sites. While they were there, the Eyjafjallajokull volcano in Iceland erupted, spewing tonnes of volcanic ash into the air and grounding flights throughout Europe, which left the group stranded in a small Greek fishing village. However, what might have been a disaster turned into, as deputy head Anne Griffiths says, 'a fantastic extension to the holiday'. They were installed in a lovely hotel on the beach and then cruised in comfort, on a brand new cruise ship, back to Italy. Alison de Winter continues: 'We were very lucky to have cabins for the overnight journey, and we landed at Ancona early Wednesday evening. Nourished by local takeaway pizzas, we liaised with our coach and drove through the night, under mountains and across rivers. We got to Calais ahead of schedule and landed safely on British soil. To the strains of "three cheers for our drivers", we drove up the hill on Thursday afternoon to be welcomed by members of the senior leadership team, parents, cups of tea and, naturally, cake.'

Pope himself. 'Just think: we've just seen a real live *Blue Peter* presenter', was how she put it. Hannah herself gave a lively account of the service in Assembly the following week.

As part of an outreach initiative, with the aim of sharing the school's facilities with the wider community, the school joined the 'Serious fun on Saturdays' programme, funded by the SHINE Trust. Twenty-five Year 5 children, whose junior schools felt they would benefit from some extra help and support, came on Saturday mornings for lessons with volunteer teachers and Sixth Form helpers. This has been just the latest in a long tradition of links to the local community, and continues very successfully.

Year 8 at Horseshoe Lake, 2011

During this post-millennium period, the school has also revived the Duke of Edinburgh's Award Scheme, now under the leadership of Georgina Brocklehurst. This was very different from the programme pursued by girls in the 1960s, where the category Design for Living had covered such topics as 'grooming and poise', and 'setting up and running a home'. It still involves volunteering, physical activities, skills and an outdoor expedition, as it did then, but 'life skills' as one of the possible topics of study has a very different flavour from the previous emphasis on a housewifely future. The provision of 'D of E' activities has proved very popular, and several groups have undertaken hikes and camps in the surrounding area.

Not to be outdone, the Sixth Form decided that they would like to climb Mount Kilimanjaro in Tanzania in the summer of 2012. As part of their preparations, they undertook what proved to be a very wet and windy training weekend in Snowdonia, and also dreamed up various fundraising activities, including a very successful 'Kili Week' in school. This not only helped to pay for the trip but allowed them to donate over £3,000 to the local Tanzanian school children to provide school meals for an entire year. Fifteen girls set off in the summer holiday, accompanied by Miss Bethia Stevenson, Miss Karen Gibson and Dr Maryhan Baker. Mount Kilimanjaro is the highest mountain in Africa and some of the party had to turn back because of altitude sickness. Most, however, made it all the way to the top and were able to enjoy the incomparable view of the sun rising over the plains below. The trip also included a cultural exchange with the local Masai tribe and some community work at a local school.

2012 was also the momentous summer of the Queen's Diamond Jubilee and the Olympics. In true Farnborough Hill style, staff and students threw themselves into celebrating both events. First there was a sit-down 'street party' lunch for the entire school community on the beautiful cloister lawns, and then an Olympic Day, with games-related activities. Some members of the school community also got a sneak preview of the Olympic facilities when they travelled up to see old girl Alex Danson, a member of the Great Britain women's hockey team, play a practice match with her teammates on the new hockey pitch.

The spirit of adventure, which has led so many Farnborough Hill girls to challenge themselves through activities such as the Kili trip and the Duke of Edinburgh expeditions, was touched on by the headmistress in her 2013 prize giving speech. She told her audience that 'Recent research done in the UK, Australia and the US showed that girls who attended all-girls schools were much better at public speaking and, more importantly, rated their own speaking skills as being in the top 10%, much better than their co-ed counterparts. They rated their skills of leadership much more highly too, and this in turn made them feel they could compete in any arena as they were more willing to take healthy risks, so vital for university and future careers.'

Certainly, there is plenty of evidence for the girls' speaking skills: the twenty-first century has seen team after

team from Farnborough Hill, under the guidance of Lori Winch-Johnson, dominating the Rotary Club and English Speaking Union competitions. In 2012, the intermediate team won first the local, then the district and finally the national finals of the Rotary Youth Speaks competition. The team consisted of Sangeeta Rijal, Beatrice Cerullo and Carys Dally, with Sangeeta, as Speaker, giving a moving account of her grandfather's dementia under the title, 'Mind over matter'.

Trips, competitions, concerts, plays and sporting fixtures provide variety in the life of the school – though for most girls in the twenty-first century, as for previous generations, the daily round is also stimulating and absorbing. Yadin Chowdhury, who joined the school in September 2013, recalls that 'At first it seemed really big but after the first week of exploring, I [knew] my way around'. Her description of her daily routine suggested the importance of food for growing adolescents: the lessons after lunch 'are probably the easiest to get through because you've just had a meal so you can't get too hungry'. The day finally ends at 4.00. 'Most people go home or go to a sporting practice, but I like going to prep because I can't do homework at home without being distracted.'

Mrs Cathy Dales with some members of the Upper Sixth enjoying dressing up in their last week (2011)

An account of a day at Farnborough Hill

Christiane, 9B, winner of a competition for this book to describe a typical school day

21 October 2013

My alarm clock pipes up with its shrill beep at six fifteen, only to be knocked out with a sharp smack to the head. When it regains consciousness, ten minutes later, the scene is very different on my part. I suddenly realise that there is a slight sense of urgency linked to getting up, and the next forty-five minutes are a blur of forest green, soggy cereal and frantic rushing around, trying to gather up the school bag, the flute, the bass recorder, the PE bag and the food tech ingredients before hurrying to catch the seven forty train to Farnborough.

I usually take the train alone, and walk up the winding hill with only my own company. However, this is my choice, as the early morning is the only time I get throughout the busy day to think quietly and have a little solitude – the rest of school life is filled with hilarity, friends and activity.

Greeting the teachers as I arrive, I disappear into the Year 9 quad, only to emerge a few moments later relieved of the flute, the bass recorder, the PE bag and my blazer. I will drop off the food tech ingredients next and make my way to the form room. It is there that the noise begins to escalate. The calm, quiet atmosphere at eight o'clock has been replaced with intermittent squeals of greeting by half past, and by quarter to it is impossible to hear oneself think. The music of F'hill Radio blaring cheerfully accompanies the screams of delight and horror as my form eagerly discusses pop groups, weekends, discos and boys. When our form tutor arrives, silence is restored until the chatter begins again.

The first bell triggers a rollercoaster to start up – once it rings, it's all aboard for a hectic, eventful day, each lesson full of excitement. In Spanish, for example, our whole class will be in fits of laughter after some 'rude' mispronunciation, and in RE we'll somehow find ourselves in a discussion so deep we have to come up for air. During English, we'll always find a way to stray distantly off topic, before suddenly realising that the bell is about to ring and we've barely even started. When that final bell does ring, at four o'clock, the school is suddenly deserted and silent.

As soon as I arrive home, I change out of uniform and take out various books for homework. This varies in length – some nights it takes several hours, others it's finished by tea time. However long it takes me, I get it done, and most nights only have time to eat, have a shower and tumble into bed. However busy the day has been, and however clichéd the phrase may seem, as I finally drift off to sleep I have a smile on my face, just thinking about how lucky I am to be at Farnborough Hill.

Christiane (left) with her friend Jessica

The last decade, heading towards the celebrations in 2014 of 125 years of existence, has heralded major change and growth at Farnborough Hill. The considerably improved facilities, the new uniform, the increasingly excellent examination results and the outstanding pastoral care have led to more parents and their daughters making the school their first choice. Numbers grew under Mrs Buckle's tutelage from 501 when she arrived in 2007 to 575 in 2012 – quite amazing given that this was the time when the country was experiencing one of its most severe economic recessions. Moreover, it is not just in the teaching and examination areas that there has been great progress. The sporting and leisure facilities at all levels at the school are now of a very high standard; the food is excellent, with plenty of choice; the common room and study facilities for the senior girls offer them both privacy and pleasant spaces where they can interact with their friends; and the continued involvement of the remaining Sisters is an ongoing link both with the school's long and venerable history and with the Catholic faith which still – even in today's multi-faith environment here – provides the glue which holds the school together and makes it so special. All these facilities, improvements and developments were fully recognised in January 2014 when the ISI inspection awarded the school the top category of 'excellent' in each of its eight categories.

And so to the future. As these twenty-first-century girls move on through the school, and on into the wider world, their lives will be very different from those of their predecessors 125 years ago, and yet the essential Christian values and belief in girls' education which motivated the founders of Hillside are still in evidence today. Sister McCormack, a former headmistress and now a member of the Board of Trustees, reflected on this when she wrote: 'Sociologically speaking, to have the capacity to adapt well to change is a sign of a healthy institution. Farnborough Hill has proved this to be so on numerous occasions throughout its 125 years of history. The school is out-standing in academic excellence and in the vision of education it offers the girls. It has truly become a leading school in girls' education and has established itself nationally.' If the past century and a quarter is anything to go by, the school will continue to change and adapt to meet the needs of the twenty-first century.

Subscribers

Jill Abbott, 1969–2000 (Staff)
Zoe Frances Abbott, 2013–
Ann Alexander, 1965–72
Liz Alexander (Shubrook), 1983–90
Biane Aliyar , 2006–13
Kailey Aliyar , 2009–
Mary Elizabeth Allan, 1945–8
Sophie Allen, 2009–13
Gillian Allnutt, 1964–71
Katherine Allnutt, 1964–71
Pamela Allnutt, 1964–71
Susan Allnutt, 1964–71
Nisha Amin-Edwards, 1987–92
Emily Annette, 2014–
Anneliese Appleton, 2004–9
Helen Archer (Williams), 1970–6
Elizabeth Ashenden (Semmons),
    1957–64
Katrina Atsinger (Collman), 1989–96

Fiona Bailey (Brampton), 1978–85
Linda Bainbridge (Pollard), 1957–63
Audrey Drury Baker, 1938–40
Caroline Baker, 1965–72
Emily Rose Baldwin, 2005–12
Lydia Jane Baldwin, 2009–
Astrid Balinska-Jundzill, 1940–52
Ella Barker, 2014–
Catherine Anne (Kenane) Barlow
    (Allan), 1945–9
Emma Barnbrook, 1992–9
Kate Barnes (Williams), 1978–85
Lizanne Barrell (Byrne), 1983–8
Hazel Bartley (Marshall), 1994–9
Elizabeth Ann Bean, 1946–52
Susan Bean, 1955–9
Alison Beatty, 1960–5
Lily Katherine Beckett, 2009–
Francesca Beckingham, 2001–8
Helena Beddoe (Knight), 1983–8
Lily Bennett, 2005–10
Sue Bennett, 1996– (Staff)
Ann Berry, 1958–65,
    1968–2007 (Staff)
Clare Beswick (Willats), 1987–9

Louise Biden, 2007–14
Sarah Biden, 2009–14
Megan Bird, 2012–
Charlotte Birth, 2010–
Holly Birth, 2013–
Connie Blanchard, 2014–
Clare (Sheila) Blyth-Praeger, 1940–52
Anitra Bowers (Hume–Wright),
    1976–83
Jane Bradley, 1981–7
Annabel Bradshaw, 2012–
Jude Bramham, 1991–7
Susan Brierley (Jones), 1952–9
W A F Brister CB, 1989–2000
    (Board of Governors)
Ann Brooks, 1971–7
Madison Jennifer Brooks, 2014–
Caroline Brown, 1950–6
Paula Broxis (Plascott), 1982–9
Maisie Bruce, 2014–
Kathryn Bryan, 1996–2003
Caelia Bryn-Jacobsen, 1984–91
Freya Anne Buchan, 2011–
Jennie Buchanan (Johnson), 1986–91
Susan Buckee (O'Flaherty), 1959–66
Emily Bunch, 2013–
Sarah Bunch, 1982–9
Sarah Burgin, 2002–7
Caroline Burnett, 1975–81
Bridgette Burrows, 1980–5
Elizabeth Busbridge, 2014–
Catherine (Bod) Butler, 1983–90

Elizabeth Ann Caldwell
    (Meacham), 1945–50
Amelia Cameron, 2007–14
Helen Campbell (Fermie), 1937–44
Johanna Cantwell, 2007–14
Elizabeth Carruthers, 2008–
Maggie Catterall , 1995– (Staff)
Cathryn Chadwick, 1975–82
Gill Chapman, 1975–83,
    2002–13 (Staff)
Grace Charles, 2008–
Emma A Churms, 2011–

Moira Clark (Spratley), 1980–5
Mary Clemow, 1953–9
Lucy Clennell, 2014–
Hannah Clifton, 2010–
Natasha Clifton, 2010–
Susan Clouston, 1952–5
Heather Collins, 1942–7
Jo-Jo Collins, 1942–54
Julie Collins, 1985–90
Laura Collman, 1995–2002
Josephine Connor, 2013–
Holly Cookson, 2014–
Maggie Cooper (Colleen Ryan),
    1947–55
Sylvia Cousins, 1966–72,
    1983–8 (Staff)
Anna Louise Craggs, 2004–9
Jessica Cramp, 2008–
Rebecca Cramp, 2009–
Helen Critcher (Fitzgerald), 1975–82
Charlotte Crowther (Bird), 1969–75
Adele Cullen, 1988–95
Anne-Marie Cullen, 1984–91
Emma Cullen, 1984–9
Yvonne Cullen , 1996– (Staff)
Josie Cunningham, 2014–
Vicky Cunningham, 2011–

Hannah D'Arcy, 2006–11
Naomi D'Arcy, 2001–6
Beth Daniels, 2010–
Charlotte Dannatt, 2010–
Carla Davis (Roantree), 1952–8
Isabella Davis, 2012–
Alexia Debenham, 2010–
Anne Debenham, 1978–85
Heather Dee, 2013–
Elisa Francesca Dew, 1980–5
Maria Theresa Dew, 1979–82
Anais Dibben, 2009–14
Celine Dibben , 2006–13
Maureen Dickens, 1951–7
Jennifer Dixon, 2013–
Stephanie May Dobbin, 2008–
Rosemary Dodgson (Monger), 1962–9

Danielle Dove, 2003–7
Michaela 'Kia' Dove, 2004–8
Anne Downing (Gregory), 1966–73
Sarah Doyle, 2006–11
Alison Drake-Lee, 1962–8
Catherine Drake-Lee, 1961–7
Rosemary Drake-Lee, 1965–72
Helen Draper, 1979–85
Eileen Braddell Drury, 1938–40
Leslie Duckworth, 1965–70
Nicola Duffey (Willats), 1987–91
Clare Duffin, 2001– (Staff)
Rosie Duffin, 2004–11
Sophie Duffin, 2000–7
Louisa Dwyer, 1995–2002

Jo Eagle, 1978–82
Ann Eccles (Moroney), 1959–66
Georgia M C Edney, 2007–14
Georgie Ekers (Hill), 1989–96
Petronilla Elliott, 1941–4
Bridget Emmons, 1981–8
Kirsten Endicott, 1981–6
Rebecca May Eva, 2009–14
Jan Evans , 1998–2001 (Staff)
Sophie Everett, 2012–
Fiona Ewart (Devlin), 1960–5
Jessica Ewart, 2013–
Christina Exall, 2013–

Jenny Fairbank (Williams), 1973–80
Amanda Farmer, 1969–76
Ellie Fenton, 2008–13
Lotty Fenton, 2013–
Zelie Ferguson, 1951–7
Maureen Field (Healy), 1957–61
Kathryn Fisher (Sellwood), 1980–7
Joy Fitch, 1991–8
Ellen Fletcher (Johnson), 1994–7
Edel Fogarty, 2007–14
Alexandra Fontaine MBE, 1978–83
Emma Forrest, 1990–7
Helena Forsberg, 2011–
Isabella Fowler, 2008–13
Lauren Fowler, 2012–

Laura Francis (Hopkin)
Amelia Freeman, 2009–
Verity Freeman, 2011–
Nicola French, 1994–2000
Diana Frisby, 1950–6
Molly Fryatt, 2011–

Helen Gallagher, 1974–81
Muriel Gallagher (Winckley), 1944–6
Ruth Gallagher, 1981–8
Teresa Gallagher, 1973–80
Rachel Garnett, 2006–13
Sarah Garnett, 2009–14
Anne-Marie Giannikos (Cullen),
    1984–90
Jane Gleeson (Caravias), 1992–7
Maggie Gliniecka, 1980–7
Rebecca Goddard, 1995–2002
Emily Golding, 2010–
Helen Golding (Sanderson), 1983–90
Janet Govier, 1946–55
Natasha M Graham, 2004–9
Alexia Emily Grannum, 2013–
Sarah Green (Dunton) , 1970–7
Simon Green , 2012– (Staff)
Gillian Gregory (White), 1969–76
Jena Gregory, 2014–
Susan Diana Griffith, 1953–9
Anne Griffiths, 1991– (Staff)
Helen Griffiths, 1976–83

Linda Hadeed, 1962–8
Sally Hadfield, 1978–81
Christine Hall, 1989–2007 (Staff)
Suzanne Hamer, 1990–6
Alaine Hamilton, 1945–52
Jessica Hand, 2003–8
Nicola Hand, 2007–12
Elizabeth Hands, 1981–8
Eleanor Hanley, 2010–
Angela Hardwick (Gregson), 1981–6
Alice Elizabeth Hardy , 2013–
Anne Hardy (McCurrach), 1961–6
Trina Harley (Walsh), 1967–74
Doreen Hartley, 1953–8
Margaret Hartley, 1952–8
Emily Jasmin Hatt, 2009–
Karen Hatt (Miles), 1975–82
Georgia Heath, 2003–8
Isabelle Heath, 2011–
Laura Heath, 2002–7
Katrina Hellier, 2010–

Alana Helms, 2013–
Angela Hennelly, 1956–62
Julia Elkins Hennelly, 1974–81
Mary Hennelly, 1949–56
Ann Heverin, 1946–50
Emma Hickman, 1977–84
Sarah-Jane Hill (Brampton), 1976–83
Kathryn Hills, 2014–
Christiane Hitchcock, 2011–
Leah Hogg, 2008–
Rachel Holliday (Sellwood), 1984–9
Anne Holmes (Murray) , 1953–9
Alexandra Hooper, 2004–9
Gemma Hooper, 2002–7
Lynda Hooper, 2006– (Staff)
Patricia Hooton (Manning), 1926–30
Nicola Jane Charlotte Horsman,
    1972–9
Caroline Hotchkiss, 1975–82
Emma Hough, 2006–13
Madeleine Howard, 1978–85
Jacqueline Howell, 1969–74
Lauren Howells, 2013–
Susan Howse (Collyer), 1961–7
Charlie Hull, 1998–2005
Georgina Humphrey (Cleverly),
    1991–8
Catherine Hynes, 2011–

Katherine Jackson-Challen, 2013–
Victoria Jackson, 2008–13
Melissa Jacques, 1983–90
Molly James, 2011–
Olivia James, 2010–
Briony Hibbard Jenkins, 2012–
Eileen Jennings (Owen), 1952–7
Melanie Jessup (Scott), 1982–9
Emma Johnsen (Williams), 1976–84
Florence Johnson, 2012–
Jessica Johnson, 2012–
Stephanie Johnston (Coffey), 1972–4,
    1976–8

Angela Kean, 1982–9
Harriet Rebecca Keen, 1999–2006
Jennifer de Kerckhove (Clark), 1942–8
Máire Kiddle (Coffey), 1960–5
Catherine Kingcombe, 1990–7
Heather Kippin, 1992–2006 (Staff)
Marian Kirkland (Milton), 1955–9
Brenda Kirkman, 1934–45
Sarah Jean Klinger, 1996–2001

Maga van Laer (Balinska–Jundzill),
    1940–50
Phoebe Lambert, 2013–
Jessica Lane, 2004–11
Lucrezia Lawrance, 2009–14
Sage Lawson-Syer, 2012–
Nicola Leach (McCrum), 1979–84
Helen Lechanoine (Byrne), 1976–83
Sarah Lennon, 1966–71
Cleo Lewington, 2012–
Tabitha Lewington, 2014–
Susannah Linaker (Walker), 1953–60
Andrea Liu, 1979–87
Lucinda Loble–Dott, 1987–93
Chris Longley, 1960–5
Angela Lowe, 1959–63
Heather Lutley (Maingot), 1950–4
Juliana Luxton, 1975–82
Zoe Lynch, 1971–8

Fiona MacAdam, 1981–8
Emma MacColl (Carpenter), 1976–83
Wendy MacColl (Sproule), 1936–9
Louise Mackenzie, 1980–7
Terry Macleod (Braybrook), 1964–8
Carol MacMahon, 1968–73
Emer MacSweeney, 1969–77
Dr Andrea Magauran, 1983–90
Kathleen Manning (Maingot),
    1927–31
Sarah Mais (Reynolds), 1956–63
Catherine Malone (Ripper), 1966–71
Stephanie Man, 1953–8
Anna Marks, 2007–14
Susan Marsh (Lewis), 1968–75
Penny Marshall (Harper), 1977–84
Jane Martin-Murphy, 1949–54
Louise Martin-Murphy, 1957–63
Elizabeth Martin (Hague), 1951–8
Katie Martin, 2014–
Anna Martinovic, 2010–
Emma McBride (Kearse), 1984–91
Rosalind McCallum, 1980–5
Kate McCombe, 1988–95
Virginia McCombe, 1956–62
Christine McCormick, 1982–7
Judith McCormick, 1978–85
Maureen McCormick , 1985–94 (Staff)
Rosemary McCormick, 1979–86
Julie McCrum, 1977–84
Anna McManus, 2006–13
Dorothy McNeill (Johnson), 1994–8

Ken McSteen, 1997–2001 (Staff)
Faith Meager, 1954–61
Patricia Meftah (Healy), 1951–6
Sophia Menges, 1982–9
Caroline Miles, 1994–2001
Elizabeth Miles, 1992–9
Rebecca Mole, 2001–6
Charlotte Mooney, 2014–
Ellie Mooney, 2012–
Jenna Moors, 2010–
Deryn Morgan, 1956–63
Jennifer Moussalli (Bullough), 1952–8
Anoushka Murray, 2010–
Charlotte Murray, 2012–
Maggie Netherwood (Sugrue),
    1976–80
Kelsey Newport, 2012–
Mary Nicol (Walker), 1949–52

Holly O'Brien, 2010–
Patricia O'Donoghue, 1922–5
Ailish O'Kelly, 1975–80
Maeve O'Kelly, 1968–75
Mary Kate O'Riley, 1974–81
Lesley O'Toole , 1974–81
Alice Oborne, 2011–14
Kathryn Oie (Broomfield), 1985–91
Jane Ord (Brasher), 1970–7
Katy Osborn , 1969–76
Sally Osborn, 1968–75
Anne-Lies van Overbeek, 1959–61
Helen Owen (Bland), 1970–7

Suzanne Pape, 2003–10
Alyssa Parker, 2013–
Louise Parker, 1992–7
Christine Parkin (Akass), 1960–5
Helen Parkin, 1996–2003
Michelle K Parkinson, 2006–11
Hannah Jemi Patel, 2003–10
Rebecca (Becky) Pateman, 1992–7
Cara Patston, 2011–
Sacha Patston, 2007–12
Anna Payne (Bowyer), 1984–91,
    2010– (Staff)
Ione Pearce, 1974–81
Emma Pearce-Molland, 2014–
Emilia Pearson, 2014–
Genevieve Pearson, 1959–66
Jacqueline Perich (Smith), 1971–4
Patricia Perry (Morris), 1952–7
Vivian Peters, 1999–2013

Cyndy Jayne Petersen (Norton), 1969–76
Sophie Peterson, 2009–
Stephanie Pipe, 2012–
Francesca Pipkin, 2005–12
Eleanor Pitt, 2014–
Lucy Poet, 2005–9
Bernadette Pole-Baker , 1970–82
Judith Pole-Baker, 1970–84
Louise Pole-Baker , 1970–85
Teresa Pole-Baker , 1970–83
Hilary Poling (Healy), 1960–7
Jane Price (Cartlidge), 1968–73
Edna Price–Allen (Henstridge), 1955–60
Susan Proctor (Reakes), 1984–9
Priyangka Pun, 2007–14
Alexandra Pyatt, 1991–8

Emily Randall, 1995–2002
The Religious of Christian Education,
Katie Rhodes, 1988–95
Alison Rich, 1997–2004
Judith Rich OBE (Gardner), 1942–52
Zara Ricketts, 2000–5
Judy Ripper, 1960–6
Diana Roberts, 1963–8
Felicity Roberts, 1963–6
Katie Eleanor Robson, 2010–
Nicole Rorie, 1990–5
Lauren Donna Roth-Brown, 2002–7
Babs Rowe, 1969–73
Sarah Rowlands, 2004–8
Yanina Royko, 1967–74
Jo Russell, 1993–2010 (Staff)
Nina Rylke, 1960–7

Hannah Sakellariou, 2000–5
Laura Savage (Collins), 1993–2000
Claire Scargill (Nicholson) , 1960–7
Jeanne M Schneider
Alison Scott, 1989–96
Stephanie Scott, 2006–11
Eleanor Selby, 2009–
Natasha Selby, 2012–

Elizabeth Sellen, 1972–9
Emma Sharp (Cullen), 1984–9
Yvonne Sheer (Lucas), 1967–75
Anne Shellim (Ripper), 1960–5
Olivia Shenton-Taylor, 2000–5
Caroline Simpson (Bate), 1960–70
Helen Sims, 2003–10
Katie Sims, 2003–10
Tania Skerritt-Cummings, 1985–90
Heidi Small, 2009–14
Caitlin Smith, 2014–
Helen Smith (Davis), 1988–93
Michelle Marie Smith, 1971–5
Monica Smith (Brook), 1944–50
Penny Smith (Quick), 1954–61
Sheelagh Smith (Moss), 1962–7
Heather Southwell (Foley), 1982–9
Gill Sowerby, 1959–64
Claire Spencer, 1992–9
Katherine Spencer, 1987–94
Emily Squibbs, 2011–
Lizzie Squibbs, 2011–
Claudia Steed, 2012–13
Lydia Steven, 2009–14
Leah Stewart, 2013–
Jessica Stinton, 2011–
Jade Louise Stokes, 2013–
Jackie Stopyra, 1972–9
Rosemary Strickland (Ahern), 1955–62
Jordan Sullivan, 2013–
Danielle Summersby, 2010
Nicole Summersby, 2012–
Valerie Sutton-Long, 2007–14 (Staff)
Cecily Sutton (Edwards), 1944–58
Kimberley Sutton (Neller), 1983–90
Georgina Sweeting, 2005–10
Sheila Swift (Watts), 1958–65

Louise Taylor, 2011–13
Sophia Taylor, 2010–
Patricia Tcherneva-Rowland, 1980–7
Mary Tennyson d'Eyncourt, 1952–7
Emily Thackrah, 2002–7
Imogen Thackrah, 2005–12

Erica Thake, 2007–14
Deirdre Thomas (White), 1967–74
Katrina Thompson (Tinkie Gleadell), 1951–9
Samantha Tolley, 1980–5
Ann Tomline (James), 1954–62
Sharon May Ellen Tsang (Williams), 1992–9
Tilly Ttofi, 2010–
Sarah Turner, 1981–8
Patricia Tutton, 1934–40
Rebecca Tyler, 2006–13
Bryony Tyler (Brampton), 1982–9

Susan Vadot (Kelly), 1951–6
Philippa Varcoe, 2012–
Rachel Vaughan, 1989–96
Claire Veillard, 1978–85
Phoebe Vetch, 2014–
Anne Vickers (Blyth-Praeger), 1940–52
Paloma Vince, 2009–14
Saskia Vince, 2009–
Amanda Vincenti, 1970–7

Suzanne Wakeley (Norton), 1973–80
Kate Wallbank, 2010–
Rachel Wallbank, 2014–
Lucie Wallbridge, 2013–
Elaine Walsh, 1974–81
Beverley Walsh, 1971–8
Scarlett Walsh, 2007–14
Isobel Walter, 2010–
Sophie Walter, 2010–
Anne Wardle (Doyle), 1975–81
Sophie Wardle, 2004–9
Georgina F Watkins, 1961–7
Julie Watkinson (McCrum) , 1977–84
Bridget Watson (Russell), 1961–6
Emily Wayland, 2010–
Madeleine Wayland, 2012–
Maureen Webber (Wright), 1928–39
Anne Theresa Weekes (Milligan), 1964–70
Jo Welling (Woodham), 1987–94
Chloe Wells, 2012–

Amy Wetherall, 2008–
Jennifer White, 1989–93
Jessica Whitlock, 2008–
Eva Whittle, 2009–
Lauren Whittle, 2009–
Rosie Whittle, 2009–
Katie Wicks, 2005–10
Natasha Widdowson, 2005–10
Rebecca Wild, 2014–
Caitlin Wilkins , 2014–
Lauren Wilkins , 2012–
Sandra Wilkinson, 1962–6
Alana Williams, 2014–
Chloe Williams, 2009–12
Christina Williams, 2006–11
Joanna Williams (Knight), 1980–5
Victoria Williams, 2011–
Julia Ross Williamson, 1958–64
Lisa Willis, 1990–7
Samantha Willis, 1987–94
Hannah Wilson, 2011–
Ruth Wilson, 2011–
Lori Winch-Johnson , 2001– (Staff)
Alison de Winter, 1991–2013 (Staff)
Rachel Wong, 2005–12
Suzanne Wood (Wright), 1971–6
Charlotte Woodd, 1962–7
Dianne Woodham , 1988–2007 (Staff)
Alex Woods, 2010–
Sarah Worthington, 1985–92
Emily Wright, 2012–
Louise Wright, 1982–7
Lucy Wynde, 2013–
Mary Wynne-Jones, 1973–9
Annabel Yates, 2013–
Katia Yeghnazar, 1994–2001
Lana Yeghnazar, 1990–7
Tanya Yeghnazar, 1992–9
Yvette Yeghnazar, 2002–9
Josephine Young (Dunn), 1982–9

Barbara (Basia) Zamoyska, 1946–50

Staff and students
May 2014

Staff

Senior Leadership Team
Sarah Buckle
Catherine Dales
Clare Duffin
Anne Griffiths
Jeremy Hoar
Tony Woolston

Teaching Staff
Denise Andrews
Alexandra Barker
Pippa Bartlett
Susan Batt
Sarah Bond
Joanne Brereton
Milly Bright
Georgina Brocklehurst
Matthew Brown
Frank Budge
Philip Butler
Rosemary Byrne
Susana Camprubi-Reches
Carole Cantor
Nick Cartledge
Emma Casey
Kay Clarke
Helen Clutterbuck
Julia Corkindale
Laura Craven
Karen Davis
Beverley Dunnage
Victoria Ellender
Laura-Jane Evans-Jones
Colleen Ferguson
Peter Forrest-Biggs
Louisa Fowles
Karen Gibson
Lynn Glover
Anne Goddard
Camilla Goldsmith
Sue Gregory
Simon Haddock
Emily-Jayne Harrison
Suzanne Hayes
Susannah Haynes
Joanne Hollis
Lynda Hooper
Keith Johnson
Helen Jones
Faye Kelsey
Vivian Lee
Stuart McSweeney
Sue Macey

Lucy Miller
Elissa Nelson
Jaimee Nix
Danielle O'Laoire
Emma Oxton
Anna Payne
Claire Peilow
Karen Phillips
Katherine Price
James Quinnell
Simon Rawle
Helena Rix
Davina Robinson
Rob Schofield
Anne Smith
Sarah Stewart
Lynn Storrie
Rebecca Taylor
Lindsay Turner
Andrew Tytko
Ralph Wellington
Polly White
Lori Winch-Johnson

Support Staff
Lorraine Anderton
Val Applegate
Leisa Armour
Christina Balsom
Sue Bennett
Roger Booth
John Burrows
Suzanne Cahalane
Maggie Catterall
Gary Conway
Claire Deeley
Divina Fairless
Sheila Farmer
Elisa Fashola
Paul Francis
Simon Green
Michèle Hackney
Samantha Hamilton
Nicola Hensman
Christine Hobden
Jacky Knight
Andre Labuschagne
Bing Li
Sister MacDonnell
Sister Mannion
Emma Martin
Hazel Martin
Tina McCarthy

Mike Mellor
Amy Oakey
Kate O'Brien
Vanessa Oliver
Karen Onesti
Keith Parsons
Jodie Pawsey
Julie Poulain
Pam Rossiter
Beverley Routledge
Lucy Rowell
Valerie Sutton-Long
Jon Taylor
Amanda Thumwood
Nicholas Tunnicliffe
Rob Wallis
Christine Wilding
Mary Wilson
Abi Windiate
Joanna Wood
Helen Woodason

Students

Abbott, Zoe	7ω	Bretherton, Natalie	11B
Adams, Lauren	11ω	Bretherton, Isabella	8α
Adams, Natasha	8A	Brett, Josie	9A
Addison, Leah	7α	Brett-Phare, Tilly	10A
Addison, Amy	9B	Brooks, Natalie	7A
Akpoveta, Heavenli	8ω	Broughton, Raphaelle	11B
Alam, Sabine	11ω	Brown, Megan	10A
Aliyar, Kailey	11B	Brown, Ruby	8A
An, Katy	9ω	Brown, Rebecca	9B
Angell, Isobel	7A	Browne, Lillie	9A
Angell, Emily	9α	Broxis, Sophia	8α
Antoniou, Victoria	9ω	Bryant, Eleanor	8A
Archer, Hannah	10ω	Buchan, Freya	9ω
Ardill, Kathryn	8A	Buckle, Hannah	L6TUR
Atkins, Charlotte	9B	Bull, Lottie	9B
Avula, Bhargavi	10A	Bunch, Emily	7A
Aye, Yadana	9ω	Burgess, Alice	9A
Bailey, Alex	10B	Burnett, Liberty	11B
Bailey, Laura	9α	Burtenshaw, Inés,	7ω
Bains, Sahib	9A	Burton, Jessica	7ω
Baldwin, Lydia	11α	Byrne, Tara	11A
Ball, Katie	10α	Byrne, Hannah	11ω
Ball, Katie	10B	Caldeira-Hankey, Ella	11ω
Bambridge, Georgia	7ω	Cameron, Rebecca	11B
Barker, Annabel	7ω	Cameron, Amelia	U6MA
Barley, Harrie	U6WJ	Camp, Jemima	7α
Barnardo, Hannah	11A	Cantwell, Johanna	U6MA
Bayne, Serena	7ω	Carley, Grace	9B
Beauchamp, Charlotte	10A	Carruthers, Elizabeth	L6RIX
Beavis, Lauren	11α	Carty, Evalyn	7A
Beckett, Lily	11B	Cattani, Bobbie	U6HA
Begley, Kerry	11B	Cerullo, Beatrice	11A
Begley, Aisling	9A	Chamberlain, Clara	7A
Bell-Noad, Jessica	10B	Chana, Chloe	8α
Bertuzzi-Glover, Gemma	10A	Chandler, Anoushka	10B
Beynon, Louise	U6WJ	Charles, Grace	L6BRO
Biddle, Jenna	8ω	Chhetri, Sharen	10ω
Biden, Sarah	11B	Chhetri, Sachi	8ω
Biden, Louise	U6MA	Choudhary, Amber	8B
Bird, Katie	10B	Chowdhury, Yadin	7ω
Bird, Charlotte	7A	Christianson, Alannah	11B
Bird, Emily	8A	Christie, Georgia	11A
Bird, Megan	8ω	Churms, Emma	9B
Birring, Kimran	8B	Clark, Holly	7A
Birth, Charlotte	10ω	Clifton, Natasha	11A
Birth, Holly	7A	Clifton, Hannah	8α
Boden, Elise	9α	Clifton, Katie	9A
Bollons, Hannah	10α	Cole, Tilly	8ω
Bonewell-Bruchhof, Antonia	10α	Collen, Hannah	11α
Bradshaw, Annabel	8α	Collier, Hannah	11B
Brant, Madeleine	8ω	Collier, Amy	7B
Brant, Kim	L6BRO	Collins, Nancy	10B
Bremner, Sarina	7ω	Collins, Lucy	11ω

Collins, Matilda	7B	Fidgett, Katie	11A	Hellett, Faith	10A	Macbeth, Abbie	10A	Pawley, Megan	9A
Collins, Emily	8ω	Flaxman, Sophie	10ω	Hellier, Katrina	10α	Macdonald, Hannah	9α	Payne, Caitlin	7ω
Coloe, Annie	10ω	Flaxman, Millie	9α	Helms, Alana	7A	Mackenzie, Olivia	10α	Peachey, Jessica	9B
Connor, Josephine	7B	Flesher, Catriona	9α	Hennah, Georgina	11A	Magnuson, Joanna	7B	Pelling, Felicity	9ω
Cook, Laura	7B	Fogarty, Catherine	7B	Hennah, Lilly	9α	Male, Helen	U6WJ	Perkins, Nina	8A
Cook, Abigail	9A	Fogarty, Edel	U6MA	Henriques, Maxine	10B	Mallender, Charlotte	11B	Peterson, Sophie	11ω
Copley, Bella	7A	Foley, Rebecca	9B	Henry, Emily	7B	Maloney, Christina	11α	Pettit, Aisling	8α
Copley, Lottie	9α	Forsberg, Helena	9A	Herbert, Madeleine	9B	Manders, Ceryn	8B	Phillips, Hannah	11A
Cowan, Beth	11ω	Foster, Emily	9B	Hibbard Jenkins, Briony	8α	Manicom, Katherine	8ω	Phillips, Laura	11B
Cowdrill, Providence	10B	Fowler, Lauren	8A	Hill, Sophia	8B	Mansell, Hannah	11B	Phillips, Anya	8ω
Cramp, Rebecca	11A	Fowles, Sophie	8A	Hitchcock, Christiane	9B	Marchant, Kathleen	11α	Pickering, Gabriella	L6TUR
Cramp, Jessica	L6BRO	Fox, Livvy	9ω	Hobbs, Pippa	11ω	Marks, Anna	U6WJ	Pickford, Charlotte	7ω
Cranham, Lilly	8α	Frangiamore, Mimi	8α	Hogg, Amy	10B	Marlovits, Zoë	7B	Pilgrim, Téanna	10B
Cronk, Alice	11B	Frangiamore, Cessie	L6RIX	Hogg, Leah	L6BRO	Marsh, Ellyse	9α	Pipe, Stephanie	10α
Cullen, Ella	9B	Franklin, Alex	L6RIX	Hopwood, Ella	9A	Martin, Hannah	L6TUR	Pitcher, Olivia	10A
Cunningham, Vicky	9ω	Fraser Hardie, Issy	9ω	Houghton, Emily	7B	Martinovic, Anna	10A	Plumtree, Jemima	7B
Curtis, Katie	11α	Freeman, Amelia	11A	House, Eleanor	10ω	McCabe, Hannah	8ω	Plumtree, Olivia	9ω
Curtis, Alison	U6FB	Freeman, Verity	9B	Howard, Olivia	7A	McCarthy, Emily	11ω	Pockett, Olivia	10A
Dalloz, Natasha	10A	Fretwell, Katie	11A	Howells, Lauren	7α	McCoy-Page, Alanna	7α	Polley, Francesca	9B
Dally, Carys	11A	Fryatt, Molly	9α	Hunt, Megan	10A	McQuoid, Maddie	10A	Potts, Florence	8α
Daniels, Bethany	10α	Fuller, Freya	7α	Hunter, Sophie	9ω	McReynolds, Tara	10ω	Powell, Verity	7B
Dannatt, Charlotte	10ω	Gammer, Sarah	10ω	Hurt, Katherine	L6BRO	McVicar, Charlotte	9A	Preskett, Lucy	7B
Davies, Amy	8B	Garnett, Sarah	11B	Hutchings, Abby	7A	Methold, Alice	7ω	Price, Claudia	10ω
Davis, Isabella	8B	Garrad, Caroline	10α	Hutchinson, Laura	7B	Methold, Lottie	8A	Priestley, Hannah	11ω
Davis, Rhiannon	9α	Garside, Stephanie	7α	Hyndman, Connie	7α	Miall, Hannah	10A	Pun, Priyangka	U6FB
Davis, Gabrielle	9B	Gasperi, Katherine	11α	Hyndman, Beth	L6BRO	Miller, Isobel	7α	Pygott, Lucy	9ω
Davison-Poltock, Cheska	7B	Gasperi, Sofia	8B	Hynes, Catherine	9α	Mills, Libby	11α	Raggett, Lucy	7ω
Day, Emily	7A	Geall, Holly	11α	Jackson, Olivia	8α	Minett, Alice	11α	Rainier, Isabella	8α
Day, Beth	U6HA	Gibb, Samantha	10α	Jackson-Challen, Katherine	7B	Minson, Tabitha	7ω	Redknap, Natasha	11ω
de Souza, Rebecca	9α	Gibson, Sophie	7B	James, Olivia	10B	Minson, Phoebe	9B	Redknap, Lucy	9ω
Dean, Madeline	10α	Gibson, Erin	8A	James, Molly	9α	Mone, Rhianon	11B	Rendall, Tilly	7ω
De'Ath, Maria	L6RIX	Gibson, Niamh	9ω	Jearey, Caitlin	L6BRO	Mooney, Ellie	8A	Reuben, Malka	L6TUR
Debenham, Alexia	10B	Gill, Cerys	10B	Johal, Herjeevin	L6RIX	Moore, Catherine	9B	Riddoch, India	8α
Dee, Heather	7α	Glasscock, Gemma	11ω	Johnson, Jessica	8B	Moors, Jenna	10ω	Rigby, Abigail	8B
Deverell, Lauren	8A	Golding, Emily	10A	Johnson, Florence	8ω	Morgan, Isabel	7α	Riglia, Isabella	10ω
Dewey, Frankie	L6BRO	Good, Catherine	7B	Johnson, Abigail	L6RIX	Moss, Suzannah	9A	Riglia, Sofia	7A
Dibben, Anaïs	11α	Gordon, Mila-Blaise	7A	Jones, Lucy	10α	Mumford, Ellen	10α	Rijal, Sangeeta	11B
Dickmann, Isabella	7ω	Grace, Jennifer	U6WJ	Jones, Caroline	L6RIX	Munro, René	9A	Riley, Caitlin	7A
Dixon, Jennifer	7α	Granger, Lucy	11A	Jordan, Beth	11ω	Murphy, Anastasia	L6RIX	Riley, Emily	9B
Dobbin, Stephanie	L6TUR	Grannum, Alexia	7α	Joseph, Annabel	8ω	Murray, Anoushka	10ω	Roberts, Isabel	9B
Doherty, Sarah	10ω	Green, Isabel	9A	Keaney, Molly	8α	Murray, Charlotte	8B	Robson, Katie	10A
Doherty, Laura	U6MA	Gregory, Maria	8B	Keating, Lauren	8ω	Musgrave, Sophie	7ω	Roche, Kristen	10B
Donnan, Kate	7A	Grewal, Amandeep	10B	Kelly, Jessica	11α	Negus, Laura	L6TUR	Rogers, Clarissa	11ω
Doran, Lucy	8ω	Griffin, Mia	8α	Kember, Alicia	10B	Nettleton, Catherine	10α	Roman, Sabrina	8α
Doyle, Holly	9α	Griffiths, Verity	L6RIX	Kennedy, Freya	8A	Nettleton, Emma	8B	Roman, Hanna	8B
Duhig, Laura	8ω	Grosvenor, Charlotte	U6FB	Keogh-Swindells, Fionnuala	8α	Newell, Lucy	7ω	Roopun, Tijana	11α
Duveen Conway, Isobel	7ω	Gullett, Amelia	10A	Khan, Yasmin	10B	Newport, Kelsey	8α	Rowlands, Lily	11B
Dyke, Libby	8B	Gurr, Eleanor	9B	Kingdom Mueller, Isabel	11α	Niblett, Rebecca	11ω	Rowley, Eleanor	7B
East, Esme	9ω	Gurung, Kripa	9A	Kircher, Freya	9α	Norat, Aaliyah	10α	Royle, Roisin	8A
Ecclefield, Sammy	11A	Gurung, Sandhaya	9B	Knight, Paige	9α	Norris, Ciara	L6BRO	Rubbani, Zainab	9α
Edgar, Lucy	9ω	Gurung, Nayan	L6TUR	Kwist, Sophie	8B	Nuttall, Amy	9ω	Rubbani, Zehra	U6HA
Edmunds-Jones, Liberty	9B	Hall, Emily	7α	Lambert, Phoebe	7ω	Oborne, Alice	11A	Russell, Melissa	9A
Edney, Georgia	U6HA	Halliday, Olivia	U6MA	Lambert, Anna	L6BRO	O'Brien, Holly	10B	Russell, Imogen	9B
Edwards, Grace	7ω	Hanley, Eleanor	10A	Langdon, Emelie	10B	O'Neil, Olivia	7A	Sanjarani, Setareh	U6FB
Egan, Molly	10B	Harding, Jessica	10α	Langdon, Hannah	U6HA	Orthmann, Celia	10ω	Santer, Chloe	10ω
Ellis, Emily	U6FB	Harding, Charlotte	7α	Lawrance, Lucrezia	11A	Page-Tickell, Sophia	11ω	Sargent, Chloe	8A
Ellis, Karen	U6MA	Hardy, Alice	L6TUR	Lawson-Syer, Sage	8B	Parker, Alyssa	7α	Scotland, Natalie	7B
Embleton, Isabella	10A	Harris, Natalie	11α	Lee, Jennifer	8A	Parker, Laura	L6TUR	Seeney, Victoria	11A
Embleton, Eva-Marie	8A	Harrison, Eleanor	U6WJ	Leney, Sophia	11B	Parker, Stephanie	L6TUR	Selby, Eleanor	11ω
Esposito, Isabella	11A	Hart, Eleanor	9A	Leonard, Emily	10B	Parker, Madeline	U6MA	Selby, Natasha	8ω
Eva, Rebecca	U6WJ	Harwood, Eleanor	8B	Lewington, Cleo	8A	Parr, Alice	10ω	Sergeant, Isabella	7ω
Evans-Wiggins, Catherine	9α	Hatt, Emily	11α	Licence, Jennifer	9A	Parr, Katie	7ω	Shafto, Zoe	7α
Everett, Sophie	8B	Hawa, Olivia	10ω	Littlejohn, Holly	9ω	Patel, Vicki	U6MA	Shead, Emily	9α
Ewart, Jessica	7A	Hayes, Lily	7ω	Longson, Jessica	10α	Pateman, Amelie	7α	Shearer, Lucy	11B
Exall, Christina	7α	Head, Claudia	10B	Lumsden, Molly	7α	Patidar, Aila	8A	Shortland, Katie	10A
Eyre, Maya	11ω	Heath, Isabelle	9ω	Lyddon, Emma	8A	Patston, Cara	11B	Shortland, Alethea	10α
Fenton, Lotty	8ω	Hebb, Emma	11α	Mabin, Rebecca	11ω	Paull, Tori	U6HA	Simmonds, Emma	8ω

Simmonds, Olivia	U6MA	Stewart, Fiona	8B	Thorpe, Alesha	7α	Walter, Sophie	7A	Williams, Tegan	8α
Simpson, Rhiannon	7α	Stilwell, Philippa	10α	Thurkle, Charlotte	9B	Warren, Isobel	8B	Williams, Victoria	9α
Simpson, Philippa	8α	Stinton, Jessica	9A	Trethewy, Natasha	10A	Wasilewski, Anna	9ω	Wills, Katie	9ω
Slaughter, Emma	11α	Stokes, Jade	7B	Ttofi, Tilly	10α	Watson, Alice	9ω	Wilson, Ruth	10α
Smale, Thalia	8A	Stokes, Isabelle	L6BRO	Turner, Catherine	7α	Watson, Caroline	U6FB	Wilson, Hannah	7B
Small, Heidi	11ω	Stone, Alicia	L6BRO	Turner, Caitlin	9B	Wayland, Emily	10B	Wilson, Hannah	8B
Smart, Michaela	11ω	Storey, Jennifer	7α	Turrell, Emma	9α	Wayland, Maddy	8B	Windeatt, Alisha	8α
Smith, Ella	10ω	Storrie, Kloe	U6MA	Tyler, Saskia	11α	Weatherup, Leah	8ω	Winter, Polly	11A
Smith, Holly	11α	Sullivan, Jordan	8B	Usher, Torrie	9A	Webb, Bethany	11B	Winter, Eve	9A
Smith, Ciara	8A	Summersby, Danielle	10ω	Usherwood, Imogen	9A	Webb, Sophie	U6HA	Withers, Georgina	8α
Smith, Kirsty	8α	Summersby, Nicole	8ω	van Hagen, Emma	L6RIX	Wells, Chloe	8α	Witting, Rachel	U6WJ
Smolinski, Laura	11B	Sutherland, Emily	10B	Van Rooy, Taylor	8B	Wemyss, Connie	10α	Wombwell, Syan	10α
Sood, Kiran	7B	Sutherland, Hannah	11A	Varcoe, Philippa	8ω	Wenlock, Georgia	U6HA	Woods, Alexandra	10α
Sorrell, Darcy	7B	Swadling, Rebecca	7ω	Ved, Olivia	L6RIX	Wetherall, Amy	L6TUR	Wootton, Joanna	10ω
Spence, Lucy	10ω	Swadling, Georgia	9ω	Vince, Saskia	11B	Whatnall, Sarah	U6WJ	Wright, Emily	8ω
Spence, Polly	11ω	Syed, Noor	U6HA	Vince, Paloma	U6WJ	Wheeler, Annie	10ω	Wright, Annabel	9A
Spence, Amie	U6HA	Syeda, Juma	9ω	Voase, Sophie	11α	Whitlock, Jessica	L6TUR	Wynde, Lucy	7A
Squibbs, Elizabeth	9α	Tambyapin, Amy	11α	Voase, Natasha	9A	Whittle, Lauren	11ω	Wynn, Isabella	11A
Starkey, Annie	U6WJ	Tatam, Elsa	8A	Voller, Bethany	11A	Whittle, Rosie	9α	Yates, Annabel	7B
Starling, Grace	11A	Taylor, Sophia	10α	Voller, Katherine	8ω	Wigley, Madeline	9ω	Yelland, Abby	L6TUR
Steed, Claudia	11A	Teo, Esther	10A	Wallbank, Kate	10ω	Wilkins, Ellen	10ω	Young, Maeve	7ω
Steven, Lydia	11ω	Teo, Bethany	L6RIX	Wallbridge, Lucie	L6RIX	Wilkins, Lauren	8ω	Young, Cecily	L6BRO
Stevens, Lucy	7A	Thake, Erica	U6FB	Walsh, Scarlett	U6FB	Wilkinson, Emily	10A	Zidyana, Camilla	9B
Stewart, Leah	7B	Thaphader, Tanzim	11α	Walter, Isobel	10α	Williams, Natasha	8A		

Index of names